# THE NEW ANCILLARY RELIEF COSTS REGIME

## SPECIAL BULLETIN

# THE NEW ANCILLARY RELIEF COSTS REGIME

## SPECIAL BULLETIN

**David Burrows** BA

Solicitor advocate

Bristol

 **Family Law**

Published by
Jordan Publishing Limited
21 St Thomas Street
Bristol BS1 6JS

British Library Cataloguing-in-Publication Data
A catalogue record for this book is available from the British Library.

ISBN 1 84661 021 4

Typeset by Etica Press Ltd, Malvern, Worcestershire
Printed and bound in Great Britain by Antony Rowe Limited, Chippenham, Wiltshire

# CONTENTS

1. **Introduction** 1
   New costs rules 1
   Background to the new rules 2
   Civil Procedure Rules 1998 3
   Family proceedings: ancillary relief proceedings 5

2. **Costs orders: the general rule** 7
   Introduction 7
   Supreme Court Act 1981 and Civil Procedure Rules 1998 Part 44 8
   Exercise of discretion 9
   Forms of order for costs 13
   Particular costs issues 15
   Assessment of costs 17
   Of protocols and practice directions 19

3. **New costs rules for ancillary relief proceedings** 23
   Introduction 23
   Application of new rules: 'ancillary relief' 24
   'The general rule' 26
   Costs conduct 26
   Open offers 27
   Estimates of costs 28
   Application of the new rules 30
   The *Leadbeater* principle 33

4. **Conduct, misconduct and wasted costs** 41
   Introduction 41
   Conduct costs 42
   Costs in relation to misconduct 49
   Wasted costs orders 50

5. **Without prejudice privilege** 53
   Introduction 53
   Open offers 54
   *Calderbank* and Civil Procedure Rules 1998 Part 36 55

6. **Proportionality and relevance** 57
   Introduction 57
   Defining the issues: relevance and admissibility 58
   Issues in the ancillary relief jurisdiction 59
   Trial of a separate issue 63

7. **Funding family proceedings** 67
   Introduction 67
   Interim costs provision 68
   Funding of the case by solicitors 74

## APPENDIX

Supreme Court Act 1981, s 51                                                    81

Civil Procedure Rules 1998, Part 1, rr 2.1, 2.3, 2.8, 3.9, Part 44 (except rr 44.6,
    44.8–44.12, 44.15–44.16) and r 48.7                                         83

Family Proceedings Rules 1991, rr 2.51B, 2.61E, 2.61F, 2.69E, 2.71             95

Family Proceedings (Amendment) Rules 2006                                      99

Practice Directions
    CPR Costs PD – Sections 8, 11, 18, 53                                      109
    Family PDs
        *President's Direction of 25 May 2000* [2000] 1 FLR 997                115
        *President's Direction of 24 July 2000* [2000] 2 FLR 428               121
        *President's Direction of 20 February 2006* [2006] 1 FLR 864           123

# 1. INTRODUCTION

## NEW COSTS RULES

**1.1**    New costs rules in ancillary relief proceedings came into operation on 3 April 2006. They follow a consultation paper and lengthy discussion amongst a limited group of ancillary relief lawyers and Family Division judges, especially the President's Ancillary Relief Advisory Group (PARAG).

**1.2**    The main features of the new scheme are as follows:

- That the new set of rules applies only to ancillary relief proceedings. No other forms of process, even though they may involve similar money claims arising from family disputes, are affected by the new rules.

- There should be no order for costs as a general rule in ancillary relief proceedings.[1]

- The exception from this general rule is that an order may be made in the event of a party being responsible for prescribed forms of conduct.[2]

- Civil Procedure Rules 1998 (CPR), r 44.3(1)–(5), the mainstay for the exercise of court discretion on orders for costs in all other civil jurisdictions, cannot apply to ancillary relief proceedings.[3]

- Offers that are not 'open' are not admissible at any stage of ancillary relief proceedings, save at the financial dispute resolution appointment.[4]

- A new and much longer form of costs estimate for the final hearing has been devised.[5]

**1.3**    This special bulletin looks at the context of the scheme, that is the general rules relating to costs (Chapter 2); then at the new rules themselves in more detail and at the new meaning of 'conduct' within the rules (Chapters 3 and 4). This is followed by a consideration of the extent to which 'without prejudice' privilege survives in ancillary relief proceedings (Chapter 5) and of case management and costs (Chapter 6). Finally, it looks at how to

---

[1]    FPR 1991 r 2.71(4)(a); and see Chapter 3.
[2]    FPR 1991 r 2.71(4)(b); and see Chapter 4.
[3]    FPR 1991 r 2.71(1).
[4]    FPR 1991 r 2.71(6).
[5]    FPR 1991 r 2.61F(2) (as amended).

fund proceedings: there is a brief look at interim financial provision orders ('costs allowance') to pay for costs in the new costs climate (Chapter 7).

# BACKGROUND TO THE NEW RULES

## The pilot scheme

**1.4**    The stirring words of Thorpe LJ, back in 1996, when the then 'ancillary relief pilot scheme' was started, now seem a long time ago. In the introduction to the 'Draft Rule' which set up the scheme,[6] Thorpe LJ criticised 'the practices and procedures by which some cases are prepared for trial'. He then continued:

> 'The underlying basis of trust [between judges and lawyers] was that … lawyers could be relied upon to prepare cases sensibly and with due regard to proportionality … It is abundantly obvious in [ancillary relief proceedings] that there must be far stricter court control together with court led mediation and a proper emphasis on the escalating costs bills.'

**1.5**    Alongside these words of Thorpe LJ, Sir Stephen Brown P defined the 'objective' of the scheme, as follows:

> 'To reduce delay, facilitate settlements, limit costs incurred by the parties to the proceedings and provide the court with much greater control over the conduct of proceedings than exists at present.'

These objectives, as set out by the then President and by Thorpe LJ, remained the aim of the new ancillary relief rules when they were introduced nationally in June 2000.

**1.6**    Judged by the criterion of saving costs – in which court control and court-led mediation were to play such an important part – the scheme must surely be adjudged a failure. The timetabling of cases and the prescribed form for defining resources (Form E) are both excellent in concept; but the emphasis on excessive documentary disclosure which is heedless of rules relating to relevance of evidence, the obsession with lengthy questionnaires and frequent failures of case management, has meant that costs to the parties have soared. The increase in numbers of ancillary relief lawyers over the 8 years is eloquent testimony to the cost of it all to their clients.

## Court control

**1.7**    Court control – and therefore the potential for control of costs – starts with Family Proceedings Rules (FPR) 1991 r 2.51B, which defines the

---

6    *Ancillary Relief Pilot Scheme: Practitioner's Guide* by Lord Chancellor's Advisory Group on Ancillary Relief (August 1996, published by SFLA and FLBA); and see *President's Direction* at [1996] 2 FLR 368. A commentary on the then scheme can be found in *Ancillary Relief Pilot Scheme: a Practice Guide*, David Burrows (Family Law, 1997).

overriding objective of the ancillary relief rules and provides for case management. Court control ends with final directions for trial and the trial itself. The overriding objective is pervasive; yet it must be a matter for legitimate speculation as to how often it is used in practice by the courts to curb one or other party's excesses, or to 'control ... the conduct of proceedings' (per the President, quoted above). Rule 2.51B contains a wealth of provisions which could make the process more economical and ensure more productive use of judicial time. Yet it seems hardly ever to be even referred to, let alone actually used – as it could be – to manage cases and to exert court control.

**1.8**    In many ways, the most radical aspect of the new scheme was the formal introduction of judicial dispute resolution into the litigation process ('FDR'). In many respects the idea of judicial dispute resolution has failed. The Department of Constitutional Affairs may only now be providing some training for judges. There seems to be no clear agreement as to what is expected of a district judge – and often it is a deputy district judge – at the appointment. Good district judges regard trying to settle a case as a challenge; and failing that they ensure that the issues for trial between the parties are clear and proper directions for trial given before parties leave the court building. Others are content to accept the parties' word for it that a case must be set down, and even resist requests to give a preliminary view. A failed or fudged FDR adds to the costs of the unfortunate litigant.

### Limitation of costs under the pilot scheme and beyond

**1.9**    The intended limitation on haemorrhaging of ancillary relief costs may yet be the most disappointing aspect of the scheme. There may be no means of knowing whether costs expenditure has indeed increased for many parties to ancillary relief proceedings. The burgeoning size of court bundles may be a poor barometer of the size of lawyer's bills, but they may be all that is available. If they are a barometer, then surely there can be no doubt of the increase in bills of costs.

# CIVIL PROCEDURE RULES 1998

### Civil Procedure Rules 1998 and family proceedings

**1.10**    In general terms, the CPR 1998 do not apply to family proceedings.[7] From the coming into operation of the 1998 rules on 26 April 1999, however, their costs rules – almost in their entirety – applied to family proceedings.[8] Thus the new costs scheme set up by CPR 1998 Parts 43, 44,[9] 47 and 48 was applicable. As will be seen, the core of the costs rules, so far as they give

---

7    CPR 1998 r 2.1(2). 'Family proceedings' are defined by reference to Matrimonial and Family Proceedings Act 1984, s 40 and Supreme Court Act 1981, Sch 1 para 3 – for present purposes proceedings which are regulated by FPR 1991.

8    Family Proceedings (Miscellaneous Amendments) Rules 1999.

9    CPR 1998 rr 44.9–44.12 were excepted.

guidance to judicial discretion in awards of costs, has been disapplied for ancillary relief proceedings.[10]

**1.11**   Rules of the Supreme Court 1965 Order 62 r 3 had provided that, in general, costs of litigation should 'follow the event'. In *Gojkovic v Gojkovic (No 2)*[11] Butler-Sloss LJ had suggested that this rule should guide the exercise of judicial discretion in family proceedings. CPR 1998 r 44.3 replicated Order 62 r 3 with 'the general rule … that the unsuccessful party [should] be ordered to pay the costs of the successful party'. It was to be assumed that the *Gojkovic* approach would survive into the new CPR 1998 regime as applied to ancillary relief; and so, it seems, it did.

## Civil Procedure Rules 1998 Part 36

**1.12**   One of the more radical ideas to develop in the costs jurisdiction of the family lawyer was the *Calderbank* letters derived from the judgment of Cairns LJ in *Calderbank v Calderbank*.[12] In commending orders for costs in appropriate cases in the ancillary relief jurisdiction, Butler-Sloss LJ famously remarked of costs orders that they were necessary to buttress the *Calderbank* offer: such 'offers are required to have teeth in order for them to be effective'.[13] Costs orders were the teeth.

**1.13**   The *Calderbank* teeth have now been pulled.[14] It remains to be seen how much the loss of those teeth will allow the unscrupulous ancillary relief hunter to plunder the costs jungle. Many more cases will now go to trial, where before these new rules the well-judged *Calderbank* letter, all teeth and crocodile-like, might have provided a costs threatening disincentive to a greedy or a mean spouse.

**1.14**   In parallel with the *Calderbank* developments in the ancillary relief jurisdiction, the same idea finally emerged for civil proceedings generally, when CPR 1998 Part 36 (entitled 'Offers to Settle and Payments into Court') was introduced. This provided for both payments into court (a concept already long known to civil proceedings) and for 'Part 36 offers', which enable parties to civil litigation to put forward proposals to settle on a privileged basis and on terms that they will not be disclosed to the court until after the trial and questions of costs fall to be considered.[15]

## Family Proceedings Rules 1991 rr 2.69B and 2.69D

**1.15**   Meanwhile, FPR 1991 had preserved its own derivative of parts of CPR 1998 Part 36. These ill-fated, and arguably mostly ignored, rules were intended – alongside CPR 1998 r 44.3 – to provide a starting point for the

---

10   FPR 1991 r 2.71.
11   [1992] Fam 40, [1991] 2 FLR 233, CA.
12   [1976] Fam 93, (1975) FLR Rep 113, CA; and see CPR 1998 r 36.5(2).
13   *Gojkovic v Gojkovic (No 2)* (above) at 238F.
14   FPR 1991 r 2.71(6); and see **5.4** below.
15   CPR 1998 rr 36.5 and 36.19; and see further Chapter 5 below.

court's consideration of costs where a *Calderbank* letter[16] had been written. Their nemesis came when two of the leading QCs practising within the ancillary relief jurisdiction (Nicholas Mostyn QC, sitting as a Deputy High Court judge, and Lewis Marks QC, representing one of the parties before the court) confessed themselves both unable to comprehend the rules:[17]

> '[83]   Thus, we are left only with r 2.69B which appears to contemplate the position where one party alone has made a *Calderbank* offer. Where the position is (as here) that each party has made such an offer, the rule becomes unworkable. I agree with Mr Marks' submission that:
>
> > "The surviving r 2.69B is incomprehensible. It is impossible to divine what the draftsman had in mind. Very often in a case such as this the order ends up between the offers – in which case, under the rule, both parties pay 'the costs'."'

**1.16**   By this time the writing for survival of the costs rules was on the wall (alluded to by Dame Elizabeth Butler-Sloss P in *Norris*),[18] and the considerations by PARAG of the perceived problem – via the Consultation Paper – have now borne their fruit in the new ancillary relief costs rules under consideration in this bulletin.

## FAMILY PROCEEDINGS: ANCILLARY RELIEF PROCEEDINGS

### 'Family proceedings'

**1.17**   The term 'family proceedings' is notoriously elusive. It is defined in CPR 1998 by reference to Matrimonial and Family Proceedings Act 1984 and thereafter to Supreme Court Act 1981, which provides a definition which comprises most types of proceedings regulated by FPR 1991; though, for example, adoption proceedings and family proceedings in the family proceedings courts evade that generalisation. Further proceedings – such as under Trusts of Land and Appointment of Trustees Act 1996, Inheritance (Provision for Family and Dependents) Act 1975 and Protection from Harassment Act 1997 – will often be regarded as family proceedings, though each of these are dealt with procedurally exclusively by CPR 1998.

**1.18**   The table which follows seeks to demonstrate this variety of family proceedings and to indicate the costs regime which covers them.

---

16   Then given regulatory recognition by FPR 1991 r 2.69.

17   *GW v RW (Financial Provision: Departure from Equality)* [2003] 2 FLR 108, Nicholas Mostyn QC (sitting as a Deputy High Court judge). Mr Mostyn's failure to comprehend the rules was mildly disapproved of by Dame Elizabeth Butler-Sloss P on appeal – for the job of judges is to explain the law, not declare it 'incomprehensible' – in *Norris v Norris; Haskins v Haskins* [2003] EWCA Civ 1084; [2003] 2 FLR 1124, CA at [21].

18   *Norris v Norris; Haskins v Haskins* (above) at [29].

## Table

| Form of family process | FPR (F) / CPR (C) / other rules (O) | Costs rules |
|---|---|---|
| Adoption Act 1976 | O | – |
| Child Abduction and Custody Act 1985 | F | CPR |
| Child Support Act 1991 – ss 27, 36 | F/O | CPR |
| Children Act 1989 | F/O | CPR |
| Family Law Act 1986, incl s 55A | F/O | CPR |
| Family Law Act 1996, Pt IV | F/O | CPR |
| Inheritance (Provision for Family and Dependants) Act 1975 | C | CPR |
| Judicial review in family proceedings | C | CPR |
| Matrimonial Causes Act 1973 | F | |
| (a) All except ancillary relief | | (a) Part 44 |
| (b) Ancillary relief | | (b) FPR 2.71 |
| Matrimonial and Family Proceedings Act 1984, Pt III | F | CPR |
| Protection from Harassment Act 1997 | C | CPR |
| Trusts of Land and Appointment of Trustees Act 1996, s 14 | C | CPR |
| Wardship and the inherent jurisdiction | F | CPR |

# 2. COSTS ORDERS: THE GENERAL RULE

## INTRODUCTION

**2.1**    Before looking at the new rules it will be instructive to consider the basis for costs orders generally, and to recall that the principles outlined here will, broadly,[1] survive in all family proceedings jurisdictions, other than ancillary relief.

**2.2**    In *R (on the application of Mount Cook Land Limited) v Westminster City Council*[2] Auld LJ summarised his view of the law on the award of costs. The comments are made in a jurisdiction separate from what are conventionally regarded as family proceedings (ie judicial review), but they are of such general application that they justify being quoted extensively:

> '**[67]**    The starting point [for an order for costs], it seems to me, is the general provision in [Supreme Court Act 1981, s 51] that, subject to any contrary statutory enactment or rules of court, costs are in the discretion of the court ... The CPR are made by the Civil Procedure Rule Committee and are made by statutory instrument pursuant to sections 1 and 2 of the Civil Procedure Act 1997. Practice Directions in general supplement the CPR and are made by the Head of the appropriate Division of the High Court under his or her inherent jurisdiction. They are recognised by the 1997 Act, and, for example in section 5(1) and Schedule 1, paragraphs 3 and 6, may in certain circumstances have the effect of provisions that could otherwise be made by way of CPR (see also CPR 8.1(6)(b)). I use the word "recognised" deliberately, for I doubt whether it is correct to assert as a generality,... that Practice Directions are made "pursuant" to statute or that they have the same authority as the CPR ... In the case of any conflict between the two, the CPR prevails. To that already somewhat cumbrous and confusing three tier hierarchy of rules and guidance for civil litigants – statutory, CPR and Practice Directions – there has now, as I have indicated, been added a fourth ... in the form of the Pre-Action Protocol.
>
> **[68]**    As to Practice Directions, what is important is that all involved in the areas of administration of justice for which they provide, including claimants in judicial review proceedings, should be able to rely upon them as an indication of the normal practice of the courts unless and until amended. However, they differ from the CPR in that: (1) in general they provide guidance that should be followed, but do not have binding effect; and (2) they should yield to the CPR where there is clear conflict between them.'

---

[1]    For a table setting out the different forms of family proceedings see **1.18** above.

[2]    [2003] EWCA Civ 1346, CA. This is judicial review case where an application for costs was pursued by successful defendants where they sought their costs over and above the costs for preparing their acknowledgement of service – normally the only costs allowed at the judicial review permission stage.

**2.3**   These paragraphs show, first, how important is clarity of thinking as to the hierarchy of the various levels of statutory and quasi-statutory authority. Practice direction and protocol yield to rules, and rules yield to statute, save where (as with Supreme Court Act 1981, s 51(1)) a statutory provision is expressed to be subject to rules. Where the incidence of the new ancillary relief costs are concerned, the gradations of provisions may prove to be more 'cumbrous and confusing' still than that anticipated by Auld LJ in the judicial review jurisdiction which he was looking at.

# SUPREME COURT ACT 1981 AND CIVIL PROCEDURE RULES 1998 PART 44

## Supreme Court Act 1981, s 51(1)

**2.4**   The starting point for a consideration of costs in any civil jurisdiction, whether covered by CPR 1998, FPR 1991 or by any other civil proceedings regulatory framework is Supreme Court Act 1981, s 51(1) which leaves costs in the discretion of the court, subject to 'any enactment and to rules of court'. The section applies in the civil division of the Court of Appeal, the High Court and in all county courts.

**2.5**   The costs rules in CPR 1998 Part 44 are the costs rules to which the general discretion provided for by s 51(1) are most frequently subject. Part 44 (other than rr 44.7–44.12) apply to all proceedings covered by FPR 1991, save that in ancillary relief proceedings (only) the first part of r 44.3 is disapplied, so that:

(1)   the whole of the remainder of Part 44 applies to ancillary relief proceedings. The remainder of this chapter is therefore applicable to ancillary relief proceedings (save any references to r 44.3(1)–(5)); and

(2)   the important provisions of r 44.3(1)–(5) apply to all other forms of family proceedings, whether covered by CPR 1998 or by other forms of family process rules.

## Civil Procedure Rules 1998 Part 44

**2.6**   The structure of Part 44 is as follows:

(1)   factors in the court's exercise of discretion as to costs (r 44.3);

(2)   bases of assessment of costs and factors to be taken into account in such assessment, and procedure for assessment (rr 44.4, 44.5, 44.7 and 44.8);

(3)     special situations – eg no mention of costs (r 44.13);

(4)     court's powers in relation to misconduct (r 44.14) as distinct from wasted costs.

Each of these aspects of Part 44 will now be dealt with, most prominence being devoted to r 44.3. Misconduct is dealt with separately in Chapter 4.

## EXERCISE OF DISCRETION

### Discretion as to the award of costs

**2.7**     The statutory basis upon which the court makes orders for costs has not changed since the coming into operation of CPR 1998. Supreme Court Act 1981, s 51 provides as follows:

'(1)   Subject to the provisions of this or any other enactment and to rules of court, the costs of and incidental to all proceedings in–

(a)     the civil division of the Court of Appeal;
(b)     the High Court; and
(c)     any county court,

shall be in the discretion of the court …

…

(3)   The court shall have full power to determine by whom and to what extent the costs are to be paid.'

**2.8**     CPR 1998 r 44.3(1) restates Supreme Court Act 1981, s 51(1) and (3) in more or less equivalent terms with the addition that the court can decide when costs are to be paid. It omits the provision as to 'by whom ... the costs are to be paid'.[3] The remainder of the rule sets out guidelines for the judicial exercise of discretion.

### 'Unsuccessful party' to pay costs

**2.9**     The old rule that costs were to follow the event did not apply in family proceedings.[4] The equivalent rule, namely CPR 1998 r 44.3(2), is excluded from application to family proceedings.[5] However, *Gojkovic v Gojkovic (No 2)*[6] – which can be assumed still to be good law, for all family proceedings, save perhaps ancillary relief after 3 April – held that, despite the exclusion of the rule that

---

[3]   See eg *Sarra v Sarra* [1994] 2 FLR 880, Thorpe J (no order against accountant instructed on behalf of the wife); and see principles for orders against third parties: *Symphony Group plc v Hodgson* [1994] QB 179, CA.
[4]   Rules of the Supreme Court 1965 Order 62 r 3(3).
[5]   Family Proceedings (Amendment) Rules 1999 (SI 2006/352) r 4(2).
[6]   [1992] Fam 40, [1991] 2 FLR 233, CA at FLR 236E–H.

costs follow the event in family proceedings, the courts still have to start somewhere:

'... in the Family Division there still remains the necessity for some starting-point. That starting-point, in my judgment, is that costs prima facie follow the event ... but may be displaced much more easily than, and in circumstances which would not apply, in other Divisions of the High Court. One important example is ... that it is unusual to order costs in children cases. In applications for financial relief, the applicant (usually the wife) has to make the application in order to obtain an order ... If the application is contested and the applicant succeeds ... if there is money available and no special factors, the applicant spouse is prima facie entitled to, and likely to obtain, an order for costs against the respondent. The behaviour of one party, such as in material non-disclosure of documents, will be a material factor in the exercise of the court's discretion in making a decision as to who pays the costs.'

**2.10**    Thus r 44.3(2) will remain of concern to the family lawyer because of the *Gojkovic* principle – application of the rule to all family proceedings other than ancillary relief – and because of its application to all other family proceedings covered by CPR 1998.[7] In full it reads as follows:

'(2)    If the court decides to make an order about costs –

(a)    the general rule is that the unsuccessful party will be ordered to pay the costs of the successful party; but

(b)    the court may make a different order.'

**Differential bases for order**

**2.11**    The history of how CPR 1998 generally developed in this area is relevant here, since it shows the flexibility of mind of those who framed the then new rules; and, regrettable though it is to observe it, it is a flexibility which may have been lost on those who framed the new costs rules under consideration in this bulletin.

**2.12**    Lord Woolf considered that a form of the rule that costs 'follow the event' should be retained by CPR 1998, but it was intended that the new rule should enable the courts to operate its discretion more flexibly than had previously been the case. This flexibility he perceived as deriving in part from case management:[8]

'My approach to case management involves breaking down the issues which make up the litigation. The court has to be prepared to make different orders for costs in relation to different issues to support the new approach to case management.'

This approach would then give the court more scope to make differential and thus more appropriate orders for costs as between the parties; for in fully

---

7    The distinction relating to 'all other family proceedings covered by CPR 1998' is explained at **1.10** above.

8    *Access to Justice: Interim Report* Lord Woolf (June 1995) Section V Ch 25 para 22.

contested proceedings – and ancillary relief was no exception – it is rare that the issues and decisions of the court are so clear that a precise, and entirely 'successful', party can easily be identified by the court.

## Orders under Civil Procedure Rules 1998 r 44.3(6)

**2.13** Consistent with this proposed differential basis for orders for costs, CPR 1998 r 44.3(6) suggests a range of orders which the court can make. The orders set out in CPR 1998 r 44.3(6), in particular, support Lord Woolf's view that it is important that the court be able 'to make different orders for costs in relation to different issues'. This range of orders remains available in ancillary relief proceedings, so the subtlety of Lord Woolf's intended flexibility is preserved for the ancillary relief advocate and judge. The list is not exhaustive and includes the following factors.

### (1) A proportion or stated amount

**2.14** The requirement that a party pay a proportion or stated amount[9] in respect of the other party's costs are similar orders. In particular, such an order enables the court to take account of conduct in a way which is specific to that conduct; or to assess a sum which the paying party may be thought to be able to pay. The requirement to pay a stated amount may cause problems in connection with payment of costs to a legally aided party given the differential between orders for costs being paid at the full private client rate: to what does the specific order relate in terms of detailed assessment of the publicly funded party's costs?

### (2) Costs from or until a certain date

**2.15** The court's power to award 'costs from or until a certain date only'[10] will be of particular relevance when it comes to costs payable following a *Calderbank* letter (so far as these may survive). From a specified date – 2, 3, 4 weeks, perhaps – following the letter the court may be expected to award costs, if it decides to exercise its discretion so to do. Four weeks after the offer was the period prescribed by the now revoked FPR 1991 r 2.69B,[11] though Singer J has suggested that 3 weeks might be a more appropriate period.[12] The order can include costs incurred from a date before issue of proceedings.[13]

### (3) Costs from before issue of proceedings

**2.16** An order for costs can include 'costs incurred before proceedings have begun'.[14] This would include the order: 'costs of and incidental to the application' a terminology which should be noted, since 'costs in the case/in the application', it seems, includes only 'costs of the part of the proceedings to

---

9    CPR 1998 r 44.3(6)(a) and (b).
10   CPR 1998 r 44.3(6)(c).
11   Family Proceedings Rules 1991 r 2.69C(3) and (4).
12   *A v A (Costs: Appeal)* [1996] 1 FLR 14, Singer J.
13   CPR 1998 r 44.3(6)(d); and see *Butcher v Wolfe and Wolfe* [1999] 1 FLR 334, CA (considered further below).
14   CPR 1998 r 44.3(6)(d).

which the order relates'.[15] The latter wording might be regarded as excluding costs prior to the issue of the proceedings. It has been held that an offer to settle made before issue of proceedings is capable of being treated as a *Calderbank* letter which an applicant could be held to have been unreasonable for refusing and that, therefore, an order for costs against the applicant from before issue of the proceedings was justifiably made.[16]

### (4)   Costs for particular steps or stages in the proceedings

**2.17**   An order for costs can be made in relation to 'particular steps taken in the proceedings' and to 'a distinct part of the proceedings'.[17] This, in particular, refers to Lord Woolf's concern that the court should break down issues and award costs accordingly. A party may still have an order for costs on the main issue, but fail on a subsidiary point.[18] Costs may go against the 'successful' party for that part of the proceedings, or there may merely be no order: for example, an order on one part of the proceedings necessarily means no order on the rest, in the absence of an order in favour of another party.

**2.18**   This type of order would be precisely apt to the conduct costs order which is now part of the framework of the new costs rules. It can be used to go wider than conduct (though probably not in ancillary relief proceedings): for example, where one party deploys evidence which is of obvious assistance to the court, but without the assistance of the other then, even though they are unsuccessful in their claim, they may be awarded half of the costs of obtaining the evidence set off against any contrary order for costs.

### (5)   Interest on costs

**2.19**   The court has power to award interest on costs, and the date from which costs bear interest can be 'a date before judgment'.[19] Thus, for example, if a client has paid costs on account, or on interim bills, throughout the continuation of the case and if that client is awarded costs, then interest can, and often should, be claimed from a date half-way between the date from which costs are to be paid (say, 3 weeks from a *Calderbank* offer) to the date of hearing. That client has had to lose interest, or pay interest to a lender, as a result of paying his or her legal representative's costs during the course of the proceedings, and he or she is entitled to seek to be compensated for this loss.

### 'Breaking down the issues' and family proceedings

**2.20**   CPR 1998 r 44.3(6) plainly gives more impetus to the court to break down issues and award costs accordingly. This subtlety may be diluted for ancillary relief proceedings by the new rules. However, in all other family proceedings the subtlety of approach available with r 44.3(6) should be borne in mind; and where issues of 'conduct' under FPR 1991 r 2.71(4)(b) are raised, the applicant

---

15   Practice Direction to Part 44 para 2.4.
16   *Butcher v Wolfe and Wolfe* [1999] 1 FLR 334, CA.
17   CPR 1998 r 44.3(6)(e) and (f).
18   *Re Elgindata (No 2)* [1992] 1 WLR 1207, CA; and see *Practice Direction of 4 June 1981* [1981] 1 WLR 1010, para (c).
19   CPR 1998 r 44.3(6)(g).

for costs should ensure that the court is fully aware of its powers under this sub-rule and of Lord Woolf's comments on the subject.

**2.21** The availability of split orders, and the fact of the new ancillary relief rules discouraging any orders for costs, may combine to encourage ancillary relief advisers to be more aware, in their preparation for a hearing, of the issues to be tried.[20] For example, it may be possible to isolate one or more of these issues and to persuade the court to make a split costs order – even in ancillary relief proceedings, and despite the 'no costs order' general rule.

### 'All the circumstances' of the case: factors in making costs orders

**2.22** CPR 1998 r 44.3(4) and (5) sets out a non-exhaustive list of the factors to be taken into account by the court in its determination of any order for costs. (These two sub-rules are excluded from ancillary relief proceedings.) The factors in r 44.3(4) can be grouped as follows:

- 'all the circumstances' of the case:[21] any factor relevant to the issue of costs can be raised by the applicant receiving party;

- specific factors including partial success (which takes the court onto r 44.3(6)), 'any ... admissible offer to settle';[22] and

- 'conduct' of all parties, which is then defined by r 44.3(5).

This list need only be noted here since the factors which arise are specifically dealt with above ('partial success' and the consequent orders available to the court) or elsewhere in this bulletin.

## FORMS OF ORDER FOR COSTS

**2.23** The Practice Direction to Part 44 lists a variety of costs orders 'commonly made in proceedings before trial'. A disservice, perhaps even causing loss to that client, will be done by the advocate who is not fully aware of the terms, and significance, of these examples of order for costs. There follows the orders in the Practice Direction which are of especial note.

### (1) 'No order as to costs'

**2.24** Each party bears 'his own costs *of the part of the proceedings to which the order relates'* whatever costs order may be made at the end of proceedings (emphasis supplied). If the court makes an order which is silent as to costs (ie nothing is said in the order defining entitlement to costs) then no party is entitled to costs in relation to that order.[23] Thus in every order mention should

---

20 For a discussion of 'issues' see **6.5** below.
21 It is disappointing to note the more prescriptive basis of the equivalent rule in the new FPR 1991 r 2.71(5).
22 See Chapter 4.
23 CPR 1998 r 44.13(1).

be made of costs one way or the other, unless both parties intend that on the particular application neither shall have costs.

## (2) 'Costs reserved'

**2.25**    A party in whose favour an order for costs is made will have costs in respect of any earlier 'costs reserved' order, unless some other order is made. The former rule concerning 'costs reserved' in family proceedings has now been reversed. The decision on costs is deferred and if no later order is made the costs will be 'costs in the case': that is, the person in whose favour an order is made at he conclusion of the proceedings will have the costs of the appointment at which costs were reserved.[24]

**2.26**    It is therefore important to note any reserved costs order at the time of preparing for trial and the advocate at trial should ensure that reserved costs orders are disposed of. It should be recalled that it is more likely than not in most courts that the judge who reserved costs will not be the judge who tries the final hearing, so a note of why the reserved costs order was made should be available to the trial judge. Will reserved costs orders be rarer under the new ancillary relief costs scheme? Orders may not be rarer. Their conversion into an order is likely to be rarer and to depend on 'conduct'[25] being proved.

## (3) 'Costs in any event'

**2.27**    The party in whose favour an order for 'costs in any event' is made, is entitled – whatever order for costs may subsequently be made – to their costs for the part of the proceedings to which the order relates. If no order for costs is made at the final hearing in accordance with FPR 1991 r 2.71(4)(a), the 'costs in any event' order will survive. This form of order will be particularly appropriate in the case of interim or other interlocutory applications or in the case of the trial of a preliminary issue.

## (4)    Applicant/claimant's or defendant's costs in the application

**2.28**    Where an order for a party's costs 'in the application/case/claim' is made, that party cannot have an order made against him or her for that part of the proceedings; the party will have those costs added to any later order if he or she is successful in the proceedings.

---

24    Confirmed by *Practice Direction (Civil Procedure Rules 1998: Allocation of Cases: Costs)* [1999] 1 FLR 1295.
25    See **4.5** below.

# PARTICULAR COSTS ISSUES

### Time for compliance with an order for costs

**2.29**    Where the amount to be paid is summarily assessed or otherwise fixed by a judgment or order,[26] the costs must be paid within 14 days of the date of that judgment or order, unless a later date is ordered by the court.[27] The court has power to award interest on any amount to be paid, including interest from a date prior to the date of judgment.[28]

### Payment on account pending detailed assessment

**2.30**    Where a costs order is subject to detailed assessment, the court has power in addition to 'order an amount to be paid on account before the costs are assessed'.[29] The court can always be requested to make such an order. If an order for payment on account is possible, then – even though no summary assessment in a case is likely – it may be wise that a party prepares an estimate of their costs, even though assessment of costs will be on a detailed basis. In ancillary relief proceedings, Form H1 will be sufficient for this. Experience suggests that between 60% and 70% of the estimated costs will be awarded on account.

### Legal aid (public funding) and costs of 'a stated amount'

**2.31**    CPR 1998 r 44.3(6)(a) and (b) enables the court to order that 'a stated amount' of costs is to be paid by a party. What is the position where such an order is made and the receiving party is publicly funded? For example, does the order come off the solicitor's bill after detailed assessment; or is the proportion of the bill attributable to the sum to be paid by the paying party chargeable at the solicitor's (or counsel's) full indemnity rates? The question arises because a solicitor is not bound by legal aid rates in respect of costs recoverable from another party. So on what figure – that applicable for legal aid rates (which is unfair to the solicitor) or a notional private client (indemnity) rate – is the proportion based?

**2.32**    For example, suppose that an order for costs is made requiring a paying party to pay £3,000 towards the costs of a legally aided party. The legal aid statutory charge applies to property recovered in the proceedings. The receiving party's costs on the basis of legal aid detailed assessment (exclusive of disbursements but including VAT) are £7,000. The following components apply to the calculation:

- The ratio of profit costs, private to legal aid, is (say) 18:7 – ie private charging rate £180 per hour: legal aid rate (say) £70 per hour.

---

[26]   Eg by order of a 'stated amount' by r 44.3(6)(b).
[27]   CPR 1998 r 44.8(a) (as amended).
[28]   CPR 1998 r 44.3(6)(g).
[29]   CPR 1998 r 44.3(8).

- Under indemnity rules, costs on detailed assessment are £7,000 x 18/7 = £18,000.

- The questions then are:

  (1) Does the husband's £3,000 come off the assessed figure of £7,000, pound for pound, leaving £4,000 plus disbursements to be charged on the wife's property? or

  (2) Does the £3,000 come off the bill notionally uprated, so that the uprated balance of £18,000 is reduced by the husband's contribution?

- If (2) is correct – and there is no reason why it should not be – then the balance of £15,000 (ie £18,000 less £3,000) can be proportionately reduced: £15,000 x 7/18 = £5,833.

- The sum of £5,833 (less any contribution by the wife to her legal aid) is then subject for calculation of the amount to be statutorily charged.

The interests of the solicitor and the client conflict over the difference between the two figures (£5,250 – £4,000): £1,250; but then as soon as a client has to pay costs to his or her lawyer, the interests of the solicitor and a client are technically in conflict.

**2.33**    These questions should be raised and be dealt with at the time the order is made rather than waiting until detailed assessment before they are considered and resolved. It may be that it is against the client's interests for the higher rate to be applicable to the contribution, it is more logical that any costs payable by a third party should be paid at the solicitor's indemnity rate, just as would be the case where a paying party is required to pay a proportion of the costs. Any proportion ordered to be paid under r 44.4(6)(a) should, accordingly, be uprated to indemnity rates; and any stated amount under r 44.3(6)(b) should be deducted from an uprated figure as at (2) in the example above.

### Notification to clients of orders for costs

**2.34**    Whenever the court makes an order for costs against a legally represented party, the party's solicitor must notify him or her within 7 days of the solicitor knowing of the order[30] and of why it was made.[31] No sanction for breach of this by the solicitor is specified, but the court may require evidence later of compliance with r 44.2.[32]

---

30   CPR 1998 r 44.2.
31   Practice Direction to Part 44 para 1.2.
32   Practice Direction to Part 44 para 1.3.

## Special situations

**2.35**    Contrary to the general rule that that an order which makes no mention of costs cannot later attract an order for costs,[33] on an appeal the appellate court can make orders in relation to the proceedings which give rise to the appeal as well as an order for costs on the appeal itself.[34] Thus, for example, if the court below made no order for costs, the court dealing with the appeal from that decision could – 'unless it dismisses the appeal'[35] – impose an order for costs below. It may be thought that the corollary of this provision might be that if the court below cannot make an order for costs,[36] then nor can the appellate court. This remains to be seen.

**2.36**    Judicial review proceedings are no exception to the general rules set out in CPR 1998 r 44.3, save that in the case of the permission stage of the proceedings, a costs order may be made against an unsuccessful claimant where permission is refused. Such costs order will normally be limited to the filing by the respondent of an acknowledgement of service. The court will not normally make any other order for costs against a claimant: for example, for other preparation work by the defendant or where the defendant has chosen to attend the permission hearing.[37]

# ASSESSMENT OF COSTS

### Matters to be considered on assessment

**2.37**    Assessment is provided for in CPR 1998 under three heads: (i) the basis of assessment: indemnity or standard; (ii) the factors which the court takes into account in the process of assessment; and (iii) the process of assessment itself, whether summary or detailed. Each of these will now be considered in turn. Where costs have been 'unreasonably incurred' or are 'unreasonable in amount' the court will not in any event allow those costs.[38]

### *(1)    Bases of assessment: indemnity or standard*

**2.38**    Rules as to assessment on the standard or indemnity basis do not apply in legal aid cases, save where a legally aided party has an order for costs against another party. As with any costs issue, those costs will be assessed under CPR 1998 rr 44.4 and 44.5. For example, the court will need to determine whether costs are to be paid on an indemnity or standard basis. Where there is no indication in an order for costs as to the basis for assessment, or where a basis other than standard or indemnity is provided for, assessment will be on the standard basis.[39]

---

33    CPR 1998 r 44.13(1)(a).
34    CPR 1998 r 44.13(2).
35    CPR 1998 r 44.13(2).
36    As with FPR 1991 r 2.71(4)(a).
37    Practice Direction to Part 54 para 8.6.
38    CPR 1998 r 44.4(1) (proviso).
39    CPR 1998 r 44.4(4).

## (a) The indemnity basis

**2.39** Where costs are assessed on an indemnity basis any doubt as to whether they are reasonably incurred is resolved in favour of the receiving party.[40] There is no indication in the rules as to what criteria the courts should adopt in ordering costs on an indemnity basis; though blamelessness on the part of the receiving party is likely to be a factor which the court takes into account.[41] An order for indemnity costs on part only of the proceedings can be made,[42] for example where an order is made for the costs of the application as a whole. Indemnity costs may be awarded for the period from the date when the other party could have accepted a Part 36 offer, where the offeror secures an order more advantageous than his or her Part 36 offer.[43]

## (b) The standard basis

**2.40** Costs orders on the standard basis are to be assessed on terms that the court will 'only allow costs which are proportionate to the matters in issue'; and that if there is a doubt 'as to whether costs were reasonably incurred or reasonable and proportionate in amount [then that doubt will be resolved] in favour of the paying party'.[44] As a proviso to this, the Practice Direction to Part 44 reminds costs judges that solicitors should not be required to conduct litigation at rates which are uneconomic; and that the length of the hearing is not necessarily an indication of the time which should reasonably be spent preparing for it.[45]

## (2) Factors to be taken into account in assessment

**2.41** In assessing the amount of costs to be paid under an assessment, whether summary or detailed, and whether on the standard or the indemnity basis, the court has regard to the factors – or enhancements – set out in the exhaustive list in CPR 1998 r 44.5(3). Where a bill may be summarily assessed and where an application has been dealt with in such a way as to justify argument for an enhancement in accordance with r 44.5(3), then allowance should be made for this in the estimate of costs; though care should be taken to ensure that only items which truly justify an enhancement have been claimed.

## (3) Process of assessment: summary or detailed assessment

**2.42** Where costs are ordered to be paid, the court may either make a summary assessment or order detailed assessment of the costs, unless a rule or practice direction provides otherwise (r 44.7). An order for costs is treated as an order for detailed assessment unless the order provides that it is for summary assessment;[46] whenever the court makes an order for costs it 'should consider

---

40 CPR 1998 r 44.4(3).
41 See eg *Frary v Frary and another* [1993] 2 FLR 696, CA (third party awarded indemnity costs of fruitless application by a wife for a production order); *Burgess v Burgess* [1996] 2 FLR 34, CA (wife awarded indemnity costs of husband's unmeritorious *Anton Piller* (search order) application).
42 *F v F (Duxbury Calculation: Rate of Return)* [1996] 1 FLR 833, Holman J.
43 CPR 1998 r 36.21; for the costs order see r 36.21(3).
44 CPR 1998 r 44.4(2).
45 Practice Direction to Part 44 para 11.2.
46 Practice Direction to Part 44 para 13.2.

whether to make a summary assessment of the amount of those costs'.[47] The general rule is that where a hearing lasts for less than a day there should be a summary assessment of costs of the whole application (or that part of the application disposed of), unless there is good reason not to do so – for example, because the paying party shows that there are good grounds for holding that the claim cannot be dealt with summarily.[48] Where a consent order is submitted to the court, parties should agree a figure for costs if costs are agreed to be paid.[49]

**2.43** Detailed assessment occurs at 'the conclusion of the proceedings', that is to say 'when the court has finally decided the matters in issue in the claim';[50] and detailed assessment is not stayed pending an appeal unless the court so orders.[51] CPR 1998 Part 47 and an extensive Practice Direction to Part 47 create a regime for detailed assessment.

# OF PROTOCOLS AND PRACTICE DIRECTIONS

## A supplementary jurisdiction

**2.44** The family law jurisdiction in general has spawned a considerable variety of supplementary jurisdiction in the form of practice directions, practice notes, guidance and – most recently – protocols. The authority of these documents necessarily varies. The first basis for judging their authority must be as suggested by Auld LJ: that they give precedence to statute law and to the rules. But what happens where they conflict with a statement of legal or other principle in a judgment? The answer to this question was explained by Hale LJ (as she then was) in *Re C (Legal Aid: Preparation of Bill of Costs)* as follows:[52]

> '[21] Unlike the Lord Chancellor's orders under his 'Henry VIII powers' [in Civil Procedure Act 1997, s 4(1)], the Civil Procedure Rules 1998 themselves and the 1991 [legal aid] Remuneration Regulations, the *Practice Directions* are not made by Statutory Instrument. They are not laid before Parliament or subject to either the negative or positive resolution procedures in Parliament. They go through no democratic process at all, although if approved by the Lord Chancellor he will bear ministerial responsibility for them to Parliament. But there is a difference in principle between delegated legislation which may be scrutinised by Parliament and ministerial executive action. There is no ministerial responsibility for *Practice Directions* made for the Supreme Court by the Heads of Division. As Professor Jolowicz says [in *Practice Directions and the Civil Procedure Rules* (CLJ 2000] p 61, "It is right that the court should retain its power to regulate its own procedure within the limits set by statutory rules, and to

---

47 Practice Direction to Part 44 para 13.1.
48 Practice Direction to Part 44 para 13.2.
49 Practice Direction to Part 44 para 13.4.
50 CPR 1998 r 47.1 and Practice Direction to Part 47 para 1.1(1).
51 CPR 1998 r 47.2.
52 [2001] 1 FLR 602, CA at [21]–[23]. The case concerned whether a practice direction dealing with the costs of preparation of a solicitor's bill for detailed assessment had parity with the rule which restricted the amount to be charged.

fill in gaps left by those rules; it is wrong that it should have power actually to legislate".

**[22]** Mr Burrows relies upon the definition given to "subordinate legislation" in the Interpretation Act 1978, s 21(1):

> "... 'subordinate legislation' means Orders in Council, orders, rules, regulations, schemes, warrants, byelaws and other instruments made or to be made under any Act."

He suggests that this places the *Practice Directions* on an equal footing with the Civil Procedure Rules 1998. He rightly points out that the Civil Procedure Rules 1998 are dependent upon the *Practice Directions* for their operation. They cannot work without the *Practice Directions*, which must therefore be assumed effectively to form part of the Rules.

**[23]** This is to confuse the fact that an Instrument may fall within the definition of subordinate legislation because it is "made under an Act of Parliament" with what that Act of Parliament allows it to do. Indeed, in so far as the *Practice Directions* apply to the Supreme Court, they are probably not "made under" any Act at all: the fact that the Civil Procedure Rules 1998 "may refer" to them does not mean that they are "made under the [Civil Procedure Act] 1997 ...". In any event, there is nothing in s 74A of the County Courts Act 1984 or in the [1997] Act to confer power upon those making *Practice Directions* to revoke or amend rules or regulations made by Statutory Instrument. Indeed such powers are not expressly conferred on the rule making body. The rules must be confined to the purposes for which the power to make them is granted. The only express power to revoke or amend other legislation in consequence of the Civil Procedure Rules 1998 is that given to the Lord Chancellor by s 4 of the Act.'

## Practice notes

**2.45**   Some case reports are described also as 'practice notes'. The extent to which the court has heard argument on the particular issue dealt with in the practice aspect of the judgment may vary, but at least the law is stated in a way which is conventional for development of the common law and practice. It will be rare that the practice aspect of a judgment forms part of its *ratio decidendi*, but it is by no means impossible;[53] and there are judgments which provide significant practice information as part of the reasoning which leads to the decision.[54] It is submitted here that, so far as the practice element is part of the *ratio* of the decision, it must rank in the hierarchy of authority above a practice

---

[53]   *Daniels v Walker* [2000] 1 WLR 1382, CA, also described in WLR as a *Practice Note* is an example where the practice issue was an important part of the *ratio*.

[54]   See eg *Sayers v Clarke Walker (Practice Note)* [2002] WLR, CA which provides guidance as to interpretation of CPR 1998 r 3.9(1). And of course the much mentioned *Mount Clift* case comes into this category in terms of commentary on practice on costs in judicial review permission applications.

direction. Insofar as it is not part of the *ratio*, it ranks alongside a practice direction.[55]

## Practice directions

**2.46**   The weariness in Auld LJ's voice is almost palpable when he concludes his words on the succession of provisions which are said to bear upon the court's exercise of its jurisdiction on costs:[56]

> 'To that already somewhat cumbrous and confusing three tier hierarchy of rules and guidance for civil litigants – statutory, CPR and Practice Directions – there has now, as I have indicated, been added a fourth ... in the form of the Pre-Action Protocol.'

A judge is entitled to sympathy when he or she is called upon to exercise his or her discretion on costs. It is the judge's job to interpret the variety of provision and case-law cited to him or her and thus to render it into some sort of order. A feature of modern family law is the proliferation of practice directions, President's directions and guidance, practice notes and protocols.[57] Some of these are culled from judgments, others from the office of the President; and now the more or less authoritative judicially sanctioned 'protocol' has emerged.

**2.47**   The weight of authority of these various pronouncements is not always easy to classify. As is stressed by Auld LJ, at the very least 'all involved in the areas of administration of justice ... should be able to rely upon them as an indication of the normal practice of the courts unless and until amended'. As statements of the law they must always be treated with caution,[58] for none have been made following legal argument and some are issued with minimal or no consultation. Others, if subject to consultation at all, derive that consultation from a narrow interest or geographical group.[59]

## 'Protocols'

**2.48**   The term 'protocol', fashionable though it may be, is open to a variety of abuse and misuse. It was recommended by Lord Woolf's Committee as a code of practice for pre-action negotiations, as soon as a possibility of litigation was identified in order to provide relevant information to define a claim and to make possible informed settlements of claims. An essential feature of the

---

[55]   A 'Practice Note' in a judgment of Booth J would always attract respect: her care with her judgments was obvious; and so it was with *Evans v Evans* [1990] 1 FLR 319 which has provided impetus, still to be worked out, for the movement to save costs in ancillary relief proceedings.

[56]   *R (on the application of Mount Cook Land Ltd) v Westminster City Council* (above at **2.2**).

[57]   For example, the practice and other directions, notes etc in the 10 years ending in 1999 demanded 60 pages in *Family Court Practice*; whereas in the next 6 years (2000–2005) they demanded more than 80 pages.

[58]   For example, the statement of the President that 'any admission made in the course of an FDR appointment will not be admissible in evidence' (*President's Direction 25 May 2000* [2000] 1 FLR 997) is most unlikely to be a correct statement of the law; and the orotund *Best Practice Guidance of December 2002 (Instructing a Single Joint Expert)* is plainly wrong: one only has to refer to the rule itself (ie CPR 1998 r 35.8) and *Daniels v Walker* [2000] 1 WLR 1382, CA at 1387E to see the errors in this 'guidance'.

[59]   For example, the group who framed the original 1997 ancillary relief 'pilot scheme' had only two members from outside London and, excellent lawyers though they were, they were respectively an eminent law professor and a district judge: neither, for example, in practice at either the bar or as a solicitor.

protocols is that they are drafted by practitioners in the fields of litigation covered – for example personal injury, clinical dispute, professional negligence, judicial review and so on. It gives practitioners an indication of what each party should expect of the other and suggests a timetable for pre-action steps to be taken. The protocols were drafted by the practitioners involved in the proceedings and therefore achieved an important measure of practitioner assent.

**2.49**    An ancillary relief proceedings protocol has been designed within the office of the President of the Family Division and appended to *President's Direction 25 May 2000*.[60] This 'protocol' seeks to give itself a higher status than CPR pre-action protocols by being appended to a President's Direction which decrees that: 'The court will expect the parties to comply with the terms of the protocol'.[61]

---

[60]    [2000] 1 FLR 997 (also referred to above). The then President, Dame Elizabeth Butler-Sloss, asked District Judge Bird to add to his work on the new ancillary relief rules by drafting a 'pre-action protocol'.
[61]    Para 2.1 of the text of the *President's Direction*.

# 3. NEW COSTS RULES FOR ANCILLARY RELIEF PROCEEDINGS

## INTRODUCTION

**3.1**    The new rules for costs in ancillary relief proceedings come into force under Family Proceedings (Amendment) Rules 2006.[1] They are supplemented by a practice direction: *President's Direction of 20 February 2006*.[2] They will apply only to ancillary relief proceedings as defined in FPR 1991 r 1.2(1), so that all other forms of family proceedings will be subject to the normal spectrum of civil proceedings costs rules, mostly contained (for present purposes) in CPR 1998 Part 44, especially r 44.3.

**3.2**    The main components of the rules are as follows:

- A new FPR 1991 r 2.71 is added to the existing rules[3] which first provides that the general rule in ancillary relief proceedings shall be that there be no order as to costs.[4]

- A costs order may be made because of a party's 'conduct' as the term is defined by the rule.[5]

- Only open offers to settle are to be admissible in the proceedings (save at a FDR);[6] and in consequence the rules (FPR 1991 rr 2.69, 2.69B and 2.69D) which defined *Calderbank* correspondence and the factors for exercise of the court's discretion on costs are revoked.[7]

- CPR 1998 r 44.3(1)–(5) are disapplied;[8] but the remainder of r 44.3 and, indeed, of the rules within Part 44 apply to ancillary relief proceedings.

- A new and more extensive Form H is prescribed.[9]

---

1    SI 2006/352.
2    [2006] 1 FLR 864.
3    Family Proceedings (Amendment) Rules 2006 r 7.
4    FPR 1991 r 2.71(4)(a).
5    FPR 1991 r 2.71(4)(b) and (5).
6    FPR 1991 r 2.71(6).
7    Family Proceedings (Amendment) Rules 2006 r 2.
8    FPR 1991 r 2.71(1).
9    Family Proceedings (Amendment) Rules 2006 r 5 substitutes a new FPR 1991 r 2.61F.

**Commencement of the new costs scheme**

**3.3** The transitional provisions in the amendment rules are in negative terms – the new rules cannot apply:

- in respect of an ancillary relief application 'made in a petition or answer before the Rules come into force'[10] (it is assumed that this means that the petition or the answer is filed before then, though the rule does not say);

- where application in Form A (where there is no ancillary relief claim in a petition or answer) or Form B is made before 3 April 2006.[11]

# APPLICATION OF THE NEW RULES: 'ANCILLARY RELIEF'

## Meaning of 'ancillary relief'

**3.4** FPR 1991 r 1.2(1) specifically defines the term 'ancillary relief' (as for issue of Form A), and therefore application of the new rules is limited to:

- an avoidance of disposition order (Matrimonial Causes Act 1973, s 37(2)(b) and (c));

- a financial provision order (s 23);

- an order for maintenance pending suit;

- a property adjustment order;

- a variation order (any application under s 31);

- a pension sharing order.

**3.5** Whilst this list covers most of the financial orders made in matrimonial proceedings, this is its limit. It plainly does not include, for example (and therefore CPR Part 44 unaffected applies):

- applications for restraint of disposal (Matrimonial Causes Act 1973, s 37(2)(a) or *Shipman* orders (*Shipman v Shipman*));[12]

- other forms of enforcement (FPR 1991 Part VII);

- neglect to maintain (Matrimonial Causes Act 1973, s 27(6));

- any financial applications covered by FPR 1991 Part III;

---

10 Family Proceedings (Amendment) Rules 2006 r 10(a).
11 Family Proceedings (Amendment) Rules 2006 r 10(b) and (c).
12 [1991] 1 FLR 250, Anthony Lincoln J.

- applications under Matrimonial and Family Proceedings Act 1984, Part III;

- applications under Children Act 1989, s 15 and Sch 1.

## Appeals and interim orders

**3.6** It may be a matter for debate – for the rules are silent – as to whether the r 2.71 regime will apply to appeals against ancillary relief orders, whether to a judge under FPR 1991 r 8.1 or to the Court of Appeal[13] under CPR 1998 Part 52. Nothing is said about *inter partes* costs in r 8.1, so it will be assumed here that any general rules on appeals costs will apply there.

**3.7** The Court of Appeal plainly has the power to 'make a costs order'.[14] Further, an appellate court covered by CPR 1998 Part 52 'has all the *powers* of the lower court' (emphasis supplied);[15] and it may be reasonable to infer a similar provision into r 8.1. It is a nice point as to whether a power – to make costs – which is expressed in the terms of a restriction, is a 'power' within the terms of r 52.10. The general rule is that hearings of appeals are by 'a review of the decision of the lower court'[16] (as opposed to the rarely invoked power of 're-hearing').[17] It would surely be surprising if appellate courts arrogated to themselves a radically different power to the court below in terms of costs.

## Interim orders

**3.8** The costs rules confront a truly ambivalent state of affairs when it comes to costs on interim orders and interlocutory hearings, for r 2.61D has always had a provision about costs.[18] This has now been redrafted and substituted into the rules by the amendment rules.[19] The new sub-rule requires the district judge, apparently, to consider, at the first directions appointment, whether to make an order for 'costs under rule 2.71(4) [*sic*]';[20] and the judge is required to take into account as 'conduct', within r 2.71(4)(b), a failure 'to send documents with Form E'.

**3.9** It seems likely that an application which is interlocutory to an ancillary relief application will be adjudged, in terms of costs, in the same way – at least in principle – as the lead application. However, an aspect of conduct under r 2.71(4)(b) is whether 'it was reasonable' for a party to pursue a particular 'allegation or issue' and for the court to consider the manner in which such

---

13 Reference is made here to the Court of Appeal, but it will be recalled that Part 52 applies to all appeals, save for appeals in the family proceedings jurisdiction (as defined by CPR 1998 r 2.1(2)). In such proceedings Part 52 will only apply where an appeal reaches the Court of Appeal.

14 CPR 1998 r 52.10(2)(e).

15 CPR 1998 r 52.10(1).

16 CPR 1998 r 52.11(1).

17 CPR 1998 r 52.11(1)(b) and FPR 1991 r 8.1(3)(a).

18 FPR 1991 r 2.61D(2)(e).

19 Family Proceedings (Amendment) Rules 2006 r 4.

20 It is unlikely that a district judge would currently consider making an order for costs on a directions appointment; but now he must consider whether or not to make an order for costs.

'allegation or issue' was pursued or replied to.[21] An ill-judged interim application which fails might fall within one or other of these categories of conduct under r 2.71, and thus avoid the general 'no order' rule.

## 'THE GENERAL RULE'

### What is a 'general' rule

**3.10** The concept of a 'general rule' in relation to costs presumably derives from CPR 1998 r 44.3(2)(a): 'the general rule is that the unsuccessful party will be ordered to pay the costs of the successful party'; and this is, of course, the kernel of the very rule which r 2.71(4) seeks to replace. The question then arises: how 'general' is a general rule? The rule-making body leave this totally non-specific. It is one thing to have a general rule, as with r 44.3(2), which is written in positive terms and has a long and more or less established pedigree. This pedigree has been infused by the remainder of r 44.3, by the comments of Lord Woolf[22] in his reports and by a steady number of cases which illustrate the exercise of judicial discretion in this jurisdiction.[23]

**3.11** To have a 'general rule' like r 2.71(4)(a) made without any attempt at definition or illustration, which is in negative terms and which has no regulatory and minimal case-law background, seems to invite litigation. For the term 'general' and its use elsewhere – eg in r 44.3(2) – implies a meaning which is just that: a general, though by no means fixed or hard and fast, rule.

**3.12** The only way of avoidance of the no order rule will be by reference to a party's 'conduct'. This surely invites some fairly trenchant satellite litigation? This topic will be introduced here, and it will be considered in more detail in Chapter 4.

## COSTS CONDUCT

### 'In relation to the proceedings'

**3.13** Orders for costs based on 'conduct'[24] in ancillary relief proceedings can only be made where each of the following factors apply:

- the court considers it appropriate to make an order because of a party's conduct 'in relation to the proceedings';

---

21 FPR 1991 r 2.71(5)(c) and (d).
22 See **2.12** above.
23 Including, in the family jurisdiction, such cases as *Gojkovic (No 2)*; and see *Supreme Court Practice* para 44.3.8 for a helpful commentary on r 44.3(2).
24 This subject is dealt with fully in Chapter 4 below.

- in making such an order the court must have regard to the factors set out in the list in r 2.71(5), which define conduct exhaustively; and

- 'at any stage of the proceedings' a conduct costs order can be made (including 'before[25] or during' the proceedings, and at the first directions appointment).[26]

### Financial effect of a costs order on the parties

**3.14**    Rule 2.71(5)(f) – that the court must take into account 'the financial effect on the parties of any order' – has got nothing directly to do with conduct; though a costs order, if made – whatever may be the basis – will plainly have an effect on both parties' finances. This may be thought to reproduce, in a sense, the old r 2.69D(1)(e) which required the court to take account of the 'respective means of the parties'. If one party remains much better able to support himself or herself after the hearing this might have an influence on the court if an order for costs were to be considered against the financially weaker party.

**3.15**    The new scheme will make costs orders against the Legal Services Commission much less frequent; but just as the 'means of the parties' must have included their ability to raise money from the Commission (if all other factors under Access to Justice Act 1999, s 11(3) were satisfied), so too the financial effect of the order will be minimal if the Commission is to pay the costs.

## OPEN OFFERS

### Offers which are not open

**3.16**    No offer to settle which is not open shall be admissible,[27] save at the FDR (where 'offers, proposals or responses made wholly or partly without prejudice' must be filed at court and, for the FDR appointment are admissible).[28] This rule seeks to overturn the long-established effects of *Calderbank v Calderbank*.[29] If the new rules prove to extend also to appeals, alongside the no costs order rule, it will undoubtedly ensure that many more cases go to trial and probably on to appeal. The *Calderbank* teeth have been pulled.

**3.17**    'Without prejudice' privilege does not go. Parties can still negotiate on terms that are privileged from disclosure to the court. This is considered more fully in Chapter 5. However, the new ancillary relief costs regime cuts across the *Calderbank* effect of such correspondence. It makes it impossible – or at least this is what the rule intends – for parties both to negotiate privately and then to refer to that private correspondence when any claim for costs comes to be determined.

---

[25]   And see *Butcher v Wolfe and Wolfe* [1999] 1 FLR 334, CA.
[26]   FPR 1991 r 2.61D(2)(e).
[27]   FPR 1991 r 2.71(6).
[28]   FPR 1991 r 2.61E(3) and (4).
[29]   [1976] Fam 93, (1975) FLR Rep 113, CA.

## What is an 'offer to settle'?

**3.18**   'Offer' in this context must be seen as a composite term with 'to settle': they do not exist disjunctively. Thus it is not open to a party to point out that they have no assets and are not in a position to make an offer. That may be the case. However, as a party to the litigation they are in a position to propose a settlement, which for the purposes of r 2.71(6) constitutes an 'offer to settle'. The term is not defined by the rules. Nor is it in CPR 1998. The terminology of CPR 1998 Part 36 – which applies to both claimant and defendant – refers only to offers or offers to settle, though by definition it can only be the defendant who is to make an offer to settle (save in the case of a counterclaim). Adopting the language of 'proposal' the claimant can only suggest or propose terms on which his or her claim is settled. Part 36 does not distinguish proposal from offer to settle, and it is likely that r 2.71(6) will be treated in the same way.

## Negotiations for settlement

**3.19**   What needs to be said here – and the point is developed in Chapter 5 – is that it is the existence of the negotiations which attract the privilege,[30] not the fact that a person writes 'without prejudice' on their letter. It is disappointing that this was not made clearer by the rule-making body. If the point is taken there may be an appreciable number of parties who think they have written an open letter merely by not writing the words 'without prejudice' on a letter. That does not necessarily make the letter 'an open offer to settle' as required by the rule. To avoid any doubt, good practice suggests that the writer of a letter in negotiations which is intended to be open should use a form of words in every letter which is intended to be open, for example:

> 'Though part of negotiations, this letter is intended to be open within the terms of Family Proceedings Rules 1991 r 2.71(6).'

**3.20**   Further, without prejudice privilege is joint and cannot be waived unilaterally.[31] There are going to be some very unusual negotiations where one party prefers to negotiate on confidential terms, and the other wants his or her correspondence to be open. The open correspondence cannot refer to the correspondence attached with privilege, but the privileged correspondence can refer to the open.

# ESTIMATES OF COSTS

## Two Forms H

**3.21**   A new r 2.61F has been substituted by the amendment rules. There will now be two costs estimates forms:

---

30   *Rush & Tomkins v GLC* [1989] 1 AC 1280 at 1299; and see **5.2** below.
31   *Walker v Wilsher* (1889) 23 QBD 335, CA; and see **5.10** below.

(1)     A new and slightly more detailed Form H has replaced the previous Form H for all hearings other than the final hearing.[32]

(2)     For the final hearing a further and much more detailed Form H1 has been introduced. This is intended, the rule states, 'to enable the court to take account of the parties' liabilities for costs' when deciding what ancillary relief order to make.[33]

**3.22**     The first form must only be 'produced to the court', whereas the second must be filed and served on each other party. The Form H1 must be filed and served not less than 2 weeks ('14 days') before the date fixed for the final hearing. There is an escape route: the form must be filed 'unless the court directs otherwise'. It must be prudent in all but the most exceptional case to seek a direction at the first directions appointment that only Form H need be filed, as has hitherto been the practice,[34] at the hearing.

## Form H1

**3.23**     Form H1 is a detailed document which goes a very long and circuitous way about showing the judge 'the parties' liabilities for costs'.[35] If that is what the form is aimed to achieve it sets out information which is of only very tangential relevance to that judicial exercise. If one of the aims of the overriding objective is the 'saving [of] expense' to the parties, then this form makes no attempt to achieve that. What will be saved in detailed assessment costs will, to a degree, be lost in preparing Form H1. The unfortunate legal aid practitioner must do the estimate twice; and – irony of ironies – the practitioner must set out his or her 'indemnity rate' where, with the no costs order rule, the practitioner is most unlikely ever to be paid costs at the indemnity rate, save where he or she can prove costs conduct.

**3.24**     The information which would generally be of more usefulness, prepared to this level of detail, would be an estimate of costs on any aspect of the case where conduct costs will be claimed.[36] The *President's Practice Direction*[37] suggests that practitioners have a duty to prepare costs schedules where summary assessment may be appropriate. To this might be added that such summaries, where addressed to conduct costs issues, should be limited to the costs incurred in dealing with such conduct. In the absence of such schedules, the work of the courts will be further increased by the added skirmishing available to the parties on detailed assessment.

---

[32]   FPR 1991 r 2.61F(1) (substituted by Family Proceedings (Amendment) Rules 2006 r 5).

[33]   FPR 1991 r 2.61F(2) (substituted by Family Proceedings (Amendment) Rules 2006 r 5).

[34]   Things may be done differently in the practices of those of the rule-makers who are in private practice; but experience suggests that it is only in a minority of cases that the court, in making its final decision, takes any notice of Form H.

[35]   In many cases it is unlikely that, at 14 days before trial, counsel's clerk will be willing to fix a brief fee.

[36]   FPR 1991 r 2.71(4)(b) and (5).

[37]   [2006] 1 FLR 864 (full text in Appendix below) para 4: 'In any case where summary assessment of costs awarded under rule 2.71 of the Family Proceedings Rules 1991 would be appropriate parties are under an obligation to file a statement of costs in CPR Form N260 (see CPR Practice Direction supplementing Parts 43 to 48 (Costs), Section 13 and paragraph 6 below)'.

# APPLICATION OF THE NEW RULES

## Applications for costs

**3.25**  An application for costs will be made at the end of the hearing in question and in the usual way. As has already been mentioned, the court has powers to make orders on its own initiative.[38]

**3.26**  A 'no order' rule for costs in ancillary relief proceedings does not mean that costs rules and other aspects of costs law and practice can be ignored. Indeed it seems likely that where an order for costs is applied for, the steps in argument to be undertaken by the applicant for costs – if submissions are made on all the relevant law – will be appreciably more detailed than before. The need for detailed submissions may be the more pressing since the applicant will be seeking costs from a judge who is likely to assume, until the opposite is proved, that no order for costs will follow his or her decision.

**3.27**  What is set out here is a list of the stages which should be followed in an application for costs, starting from the proposition that the 'general rule' is that 'the court will not make an order requiring one party to pay the costs of another party' in ancillary relief proceedings.[39] However, it must always be borne in mind always that the rule is only a 'general' rule in the sense that the r 44.3(2) costs rule[40] is a general rule. It can always be displaced for reasons – and conduct is the only one specifically referred to in the rules – of similar weight to those found by the court under r 44.3 not to provide for costs following the event. And, it must be said, an order for no order for costs was probably the most usual disposal on costs outside the Principal Registry of the Family Division, and, perhaps, in parts of South-East England.

## Hierarchy of costs provisions

**3.28**  The list of statutory and other regulatory provisions – more accurately perhaps, a hierarchy – applicable to orders for costs was explained by Auld LJ in the Court of Appeal in *R (on the application of Mount Cook Land Limited) v Westminster City Council*[41] as follows:

> '**[67]**  The starting point, it seems to me, is the general provision in [Supreme Court Act 1981, s 51] that, subject to any contrary statutory enactment or rules of court, costs are in the discretion of the court … The CPR are made by the Civil Procedure Rule Committee and are made by statutory instrument pursuant to sections 1 and 2 of the Civil Procedure Act 1997. Practice Directions in general supplement the CPR and are made by the Head of the appropriate Division of the High Court under his or her inherent jurisdiction. They are recognised by the 1997 Act, and, for example in section 5(1) and Schedule 1, paragraphs 3 and 6, may in certain

---

38   See **2.4** above, and Chapter 4 for costs orders for misconduct and wasted costs.
39   FPR 1991 r 2.71(4)(a).
40   That the unsuccessful party pays the successful party's costs.
41   [2003] EWCA Civ 1346, CA at [67].

circumstances have the effect of provisions that could otherwise be made by way of CPR (see also CPR 8.1(6)(b)). I use the word "recognised" deliberately, for I doubt whether it is correct to assert as a generality, ... that Practice Directions are made "pursuant" to statute or that they have the same authority as the CPR ... In the case of any conflict between the two, the CPR prevails. To that already somewhat cumbrous and confusing three tier hierarchy of rules and guidance for civil litigants – statutory, CPR and Practice Directions – there has now, as I have indicated, been added a fourth ... in the form of the Pre-Action Protocol.'

## A six-stage test in ancillary relief proceedings

**3.29** If Auld LJ's analysis is applied to the ancillary relief jurisdiction, and this is done in the light of FPR 1991 r 2.71, the stages in an application for costs are as follows:

(1) Supreme Court Act 1981, s 51, as ever, which leaves costs in the discretion of the court, subject to 'any enactment and to rules of court' (s 51(1)).

(2) In ancillary relief proceedings (only) CPR 1998 r 44.3(1)–(5) is disapplied, and the 'general rule' is that there should be no order for costs. If no order is to be made, then that ends the matter. If the court decides to make an order it can do so on one of two bases:

   (i) by saying it does not intend to follow – it will depart from – the 'general rule';[42] or
   (ii) on grounds of 'conduct'.[43]

(3) If the court decides not to follow the general rule other than on grounds of 'conduct', it finds itself back with discretion under Supreme Court Act 1981, s 51(1); and that discretion is in no way confined by rules, such as CPR 1998 r 44.3(3).

(4) The court may make an order based on 'conduct' as defined by r 2.71(4)(b) and (5).

(5) There are a variety of practice directions and other guidance, notes and President's directions to which ancillary relief proceedings are subject. ('Amongst costs conduct is failure to comply ... with any practice direction'.)[44] The CPR 1998 *Costs Practice Direction* continues to apply (Section 8 applies to the exercise of the court's discretion on costs and CPR 1998 r 44.3).[45]

---

[42] See **3.31** below.
[43] FPR 1991 r 2.71(4)(b).
[44] FPR 1991 r 2.71(5)(a).
[45] It seems inevitable that Section 8 will continue to be applied by courts and practitioners, even though the main operative parts of r 44.3 are not intended to apply to r 2.71.

(6)      Finally, it may be thought that the Ancillary Relief Protocol, to which all ancillary relief applications are said to be subject, should be considered. Under that the court can visit with 'consequences' a party who does not comply with it;[46] though as yet these consequences are undefined.

**3.30**   So there will be a six-stage test for any order for costs, and it is at stage (4) – and occasionally stage (3) – that the battles will be fought. The rules which apply there replace the old relatively straightforward combination of CPR 1998 r 44.3 (with all its flexibility as explained above)[47] and FPR 1991 rr 2.69B and 2.69D. Instead, to obtain an order for costs it will generally be necessary to persuade a court that there has been conduct of such an extent, within the terms of the list at r 2.71(5), that an order for costs should be made. This is the subject of the next chapter.

## Departure from the 'general rule'

**3.31**   The drafting of r 2.71(4) makes it clear that the conduct costs route under r 2.71(4)(b) is but one of the routes available to the court when it exercises its discretion in ancillary relief cases to depart from the r 2.71(4)(a) 'general rule'. As can be seen, r 2.71(4)(b) is written in permissive terms. CPR 1998 r 44.3(1)–(5) is not an option since this 'shall not apply to ancillary relief proceedings'.[48] The court will then be thrown back upon Supreme Court Act 1981, s 51(1) and will, it seems, be permitted to exercise unfettered discretion. It is likely, despite this, that any judge faced with such freedom will fall back – albeit not openly – upon r 44.3(4) and (5).

## Applications for costs

**3.32**   The trigger for an order for costs is generally the application at the end of a hearing of one or other party; and generally that is how a costs order will be made. However, Supreme Court Act 1981, s 51(3) makes it clear that orders can be made of the court's own motion: the court has 'full power to determine by whom and to what extent the costs [of any proceedings] are to be paid'. Whilst the majority of costs orders will therefore derive from the one or other party's application, it is clear that the court has a discretion to proceed on its own initiative. For example:

(1)      CPR 1998 r 44.14[49] enables the court to make an order where 'it appears to the court' that the behaviour of a party or his legal representative has amounted to misconduct: that is to say that their 'conduct [has been] unreasonable or improper';[50] and

---

[46]   *President's Direction of 25 May 2000* [2000] 1 FLR 997: Ancillary Relief Protocol at para 1.3.
[47]   See **2.8** above.
[48]   FPR 1991 r 2.71(1).
[49]   The rule is described as the 'Court's powers in relation to misconduct': see **4.24** for further consideration of this rule.
[50]   CPR 1998 r 44.14(1)(b).

(2)     Supreme Court Act 1981, s 51(6) (wasted costs)[51] is framed in terms that enables the 'court [to] disallow, or … order' payment or disallowance of wasted costs.

**3.33**     The existence of this power in the court may prove significant under the new rules. The court may be aware of 'conduct' – in that much of the perception of that conduct in the final analysis will rest with the judge – where the parties are not conscious of it in quite the same way. An order for costs in ancillary relief proceedings can only be made where the court decides not to follow the general rule; or where conduct costs or other misconduct is in issue.[52] If a judge does decide to make an order on his or her own initiative, the availability of such orders is as follows:

(1)     a conventional conduct costs order;[53]

(2)     an order related to the 'misconduct' of a party or the party's legal representative;[54] or

(3)     a wasted costs order.[55]

**3.34**     If the court makes an order for costs under (1) it will need to decide whether the costs are to be assessed and paid on the indemnity[56] or the standard basis. Orders under (2) or (3) are likely to be on the indemnity basis.[57] Whether or not a wasted costs or a misconduct order are to be made will be considered in the next chapter.

## THE *LEADBEATER* PRINCIPLE

### *Leadbeater* after the no costs order rule

**3.35**     In *GW v RW (Financial Provision: Departure from Equality)*[58] Mr Nicholas Mostyn QC considered the hypothetical question of what might be the position on the incidence of a no costs order principle on a party's assets, in the following terms:

> '**[101]**     It seems to me that if the starting point is no order as to costs then the *Leadbeater*[59] technique should be abandoned. Costs paid should not be added back, and costs outstanding should be included as a debt in the schedule of assets.'

---

[51]   See further Chapter 7.
[52]   Dealt with in Chapter 4.
[53]   FPR 1991 r 2.71(4)(b); and see Chapter 4.
[54]   CPR 1998 r 44.14; and see Chapter 4.
[55]   Supreme Court Act 1981, s 51(6); CPR 1998 r 48.7; and see Chapter 4.
[56]   See further **2.38** above.
[57]   Considered fully at **4.7** below.
[58]   [2003] 2 FLR 108, Nicholas Mostyn QC sitting as a Deputy High Court judge.
[59]   *Leadbeater v Leadbeater* [1989] FLR 789, Balcombe J at 790.

The *Leadbeater* principle or technique requires the court to credit back into the couple's assets any costs already paid to their solicitors for the reasons explained by Balcombe J below.

**3.36** Mr Mostyn's judicial reasoning seems to have influenced the views of the committee which framed the new rules. It may therefore be instructive to consider what Balcombe J (as he then was) actually said in *Leadbeater*, then to look at several of the modern cases where the point has been judicially considered. Next, the principle must be looked at in the light of the law as it seems likely to be after 3 April 2006. Finally, it is important not to overlook the practical questions which may weigh on the exercise of judicial discretion. Judicial dicta will be quoted relatively fully since this aspect of the incidence of the new rules justifies careful consideration.

## *Leadbeater*

**3.37** In *Leadbeater* Balcombe J was dealing with a case in which, relative to the parties' assets, large amounts of money had been spent on the family litigation (including in respect of children proceedings). Both parties were paying privately and both had paid different proportions of their total costs liability to their lawyers. The question then was how that costs liability and the payments already made should be treated. Balcombe J dealt with this question as follows:

> 'Before I turn to the question of the parties' assets and income and earning capacity, there is one general point which I need to deal with, because it has a considerable effect on this case. That is the incidence of costs on the parties' assets and liabilities.
>
> In accordance with the practice direction, estimates of costs have been given, and the question is how should they be taken into account, this being a case where neither side is legally aided. The wife's estimated costs of this case total £35,000, of which she has already paid some £13,000 and has a contingent, or actual, liability for the balance of £22,000. (In all cases I am giving round figures; the precise figures are irrelevant for this purpose.) The husband's total costs have been estimated at £23,000 and this liability has been estimated at the sum of £15,100, but that includes a figure for some part of the costs which he owes his former wife in the other proceedings.
>
> The question of principle which arises here is how should I treat these costs in estimating the assets of the parties, and in particular those of the wife's in finding what she has available for her needs?
>
> Mr Marks, for the husband, has submitted to me that I should add back into the assets of each party what has already been paid by that party on account of costs, less only such part of that figure that has already been paid that would never, in any event, be recoverable, in particular, of course, the difference between a figure for solicitor and own client costs and what might be recovered on taxation by way of an order for party and party costs, subject to the further gloss that there should be deducted any part of that element (i.e. the difference between solicitor and own client and party and party costs) that may have been incurred unreasonably. On

the same basis, he submits, one should omit from the party's liabilities any future liability for costs except, again, such part of that future liability as might properly never be recoverable. The reason for that submission, which seems to me to be sound and to which Mr Feder [for the wife] was unable to advance any answer which I found satisfactory, is this. If, in estimating the wife's present capital position, and in particular what money she has available to buy a house, I left out of account the money she has already spent on account of costs and deducted her future liability to her solicitors for her costs (I am talking now of party and party costs) then, whatever order I might eventually make by way of an order for costs – and, of course, as yet I have heard no argument on costs – I would be anticipating that order. If I found that, because of the costs that have already been paid and the future liability for costs, the wife's assets are so depleted that to give her the sort of house that she reasonably requires the husband has got to pay her (by way of example) some £10,000, £15,000 or £20,000 (it matters not for this purpose), I would virtually be anticipating any order for costs that would otherwise be made, and that must be wrong ...

[W]here, as here, the figures, as will be come apparent, are such that even if costs are taken into account in the way that I have stated, there would be enough for the wife to live (although not to the same standard as if the costs had not been taken into account), then it does seem to me right and proper that I should give effect to this submission by Mr Marks, and I do so.'

## *Leadbeater* in 2004: Wilson J

**3.38**     The question arose again more recently in *S v B (Ancillary Relief: Costs)*[60] where Wilson J (as he then was) heard an appeal from a district judge of the Principal Registry. At the time of the hearing below the wife's total outstanding legal costs were £121,000; the husband's were £55,000. Between them they had already paid more than £100,000 on account of those costs. In part, the level of costs was attributable to an investigation insisted upon by the wife into loan repayments from the husband to his parents.[61] Ultimately the district judge had concluded that these repayments were genuine. He awarded the wife a lump sum representing 66% of the net proceeds of sale of the matrimonial home, or £465,000, whichever was the higher (with the expectation, on the current valuation, that the wife would receive £475,000), ordered the husband to make nominal periodical payments for an extendable period of 10 years, and decided that there should be no order for costs between the parties.

**3.39**     The husband's appeal included an appeal on the question of costs. On this issue Wilson J allowed the appeal and awarded costs as a charge on the wife's property:

'**[45]**   ... I believe that, when he made no order as to costs, the judge was proceeding on the usual, but in this case invalid, assumption that the effect

---

60   [2004] EWHC 2089 (Fam), [2005] 1 FLR 474, Wilson J (as he then was).
61   Under the new rules this enquiry – described by the judge as a 'reckless obstinacy' – must surely attract an order for conduct costs (eg r 2.71(5)(c)); and see **4.5** et seq below.

would be that the wife would bear her own costs. He momentarily forgot that, by virtue of other orders referable not to principle but to practicality, the husband was already paying at least all the wife's costs on the standard basis. In truth the effect of his making no order as to costs was not to punish the wife for her error in pursuing an issue: it was to punish the husband.

[46] I conclude, therefore, that I must exercise afresh the judge's discretion referable to costs. In this respect Mr Scott seeks to some extent to justify the wife's stance in relation to the husband's payments to his parents. He submits that, whatever the outcome, a wife is entitled to be suspicious of substantial payments made by a husband when his marriage is breaking down. But, whatever the extent of the husband's wealth, the extreme shortness of the marriage placed a low ceiling, referable only to need, upon this wife's recovery. And there was a reckless obstinacy about the wife's assertions which led Mr Scott to arrive at court as heir to two unarguable formulations of her case and an equally misconceived application for an order setting dispositions aside. I hold that it was reasonable for the wife during the assembly of the case for hearing to have conducted some enquiry – and thus to have incurred some expense – in relation to the payments; but the enquiry – and thus the costs on both sides – became completely out of proportion. When I add this feature to my analysis of the *Calderbank* correspondence, I am driven to the conclusion that it would be wrong to leave undisturbed the effect of other orders which oblige the husband to pay all the wife's costs on the standard basis.

[47]   There is no question of my making an award of costs to the husband which would entitle him to set any part of it off against the lump sum payable to the wife, whatever pursuant to the judge's order such may prove to be. Notwithstanding the current valuation of the home, a set-off would, on any view, place in some jeopardy the purchase (inclusive of collateral costs such as stamp duty at 3%) of reasonable three-bedroom accommodation for the child and thus for the wife. So I am thrown back upon a charge, for which I share the judge's lack of enthusiasm. Nevertheless to say of a litigant 'since she cannot pay him now, she should never pay him' is to stand justice on her head.

[48]   The judge's instinct, if not his order, was right, namely that – truly – there should have been no order as to the costs of the financial proceedings between the parties. There will be a charge in favour of the husband over the wife's new home in the proportion that £112,000 bears to its purchase price. [*The judge then dealt with 'the triggers for enforcement of the charge' and other factors which should be covered in the charge.*]

[49]   This appeal is an excellent advertisement for the radical reforms suggested by the costs sub-committee, chaired by Bodey J, of the President's Ancillary Relief Advisory Group, to which reference was made by Thorpe LJ in *Norris v Norris; Haskins v Haskins* [2003] EWCA Civ 1084, [2003] 1 WLR 2960, [2003] 2 FLR 1124 at [64] and which are said to be close to introduction by rule. Once the *Bodey* reforms take effect, the general principle will apparently be to the effect that there should be no order as to costs between the parties in the absence of unreasonable conduct in relation to the proceedings. Of at least equal significance, if duly

introduced, will be the suggested provision that no without prejudice offer can be taken into account in any determination as to costs. The consignment to history of *Calderbank* correspondence in proceedings for ancillary relief and thus the emergence of an ability to treat a party's outstanding costs as one of his liabilities definitively within the substantive judgment, ie without the need or indeed opportunity for such subsequent consideration as may demand that their earlier treatment be undermined, is hugely attractive. Such is demonstrated by the present case, in which the judge fell against what can best be described as a trip-wire.'

## A reconsideration of *Leadbeater*

**3.40**   And so back to Mr Nicholas Mostyn QC in *GW v RW (Financial Provision: Departure from Equality)*,[62] where it will be recalled that both he and Mr Marks QC professed to find the then ancillary relief costs rules 'incomprehensible'. There Mr Mostyn dealt with *Leadbeater* as follows:

'**[99]**   If my suggestion[63] is to be adopted then there will have to be a reconsideration of the *Leadbeater* technique of adding back the costs expended by the parties into the schedule of assets. It can be seen that I have done this, with the parties' assent, in the schedule of assets at para [20] above. The logic of *Leadbeater* cannot be gainsaid, namely, that not to add back costs paid, and not to deduct costs outstanding, effectively pre-empts the court's decision as to costs. But it is plainly an artifice, for the costs paid are gone and the costs outstanding will assuredly be recovered by the parties' solicitors. Costs paid do not exist as an asset, and costs outstanding are as much a debt as a debt due to any other creditor.

**[100]**   In *Wells v Wells* [2002] EWCA Civ 476, [2002] 2 FLR 97, Thorpe LJ casts doubt on the *Leadbeater* technique. He said at para [31]:

"Finally, we record Mr Posnansky's supplemental submission that the judge should not have added back the costs spent, applying the practice established in *Leadbeater v Leadbeater* [1985] FLR 789 (*Leadbeater*). The practice was introduced on the premise that the assessment of an applicant's needs without both adding back payments made and disregarding liability for unpaid costs incurred and to be incurred, would effectively anticipate the costs order that would eventually be made. However, in this modern world of time costing and departmental targets, few if any, litigate on credit. In reality solicitors require to be put in funds either in advance of each step along the litigation road or soon thereafter. There is therefore an artificiality in the practice and judges must be careful not to lose sight of the reality. In the husband's case the money was spent and was most unlikely to be his to spend again. In the wife's case the money was spent and might be recovered in whole or in part dependent on negotiations that might have been conducted in *Calderbank* correspondence. That of course was only the wife's due if

---

[62]   [2003] 2 FLR 108 at [83]; and see **1.15** above.

[63]   '[A] safer starting point nowadays in a big money case, where the assets exceed the aggregate of the parties' needs, is that there should be no order as to costs' (para [92]).

she had been pushed all the way to trial by the husband's failure to negotiate realistically. In the present case we are quite satisfied that Wilson J never lost sight of these realities and we therefore reject the submission. However the adoption of the *Leadbeater* mechanism should never be automatic. It is probably more useful in cases where one party has paid money out and the other has obtained credit by offering security or where the court suspects some element of contrivance or artificiality in the arrangements which one party has set up."

[101]   It seems to me that if the starting point is no order as to costs then the *Leadbeater* technique should be abandoned. Costs paid should not be added back, and costs outstanding should be included as a debt in the schedule of assets.'

## Costs: an exercise of discretion

**3.41**   Before these judicial pronouncements can be considered and their consequences examined, it is necessary to return to the legislative framework.[64] Any order for costs is a matter for the court's discretion, as is the court's disposal of all ancillary relief claims. The extent to which it considers the parties assets is framed by the factors in Matrimonial Causes Act 1973, s 25(1) and (2); but in reality these give the court enormous flexibility and a generous pallet. The consequence of the *Leadbeater* approach is that the two discretionary exercises must be balanced in this area, for to ignore the question of payments on account of costs skews the way in which the s 25 exercise works out.

**3.42**   Since costs and ancillary relief disposal are, thus, quintessentially areas for the exercise of individual judicial discretion, it must be clearly recalled that the comments of any of the judges cited above are no more than persuasive in any particular case. Each judge, when he or she exercises an individual discretion on costs or ancillary relief disposal, is entitled to give such weight as each of them considers appropriate to each of these judicial comments.

**3.43**   So on *Leadbeater* Mr Mostyn opines as follows:

'The logic of *Leadbeater* cannot be gainsaid, namely, that not to add back costs paid, and not to deduct costs outstanding, effectively pre-empts the court's decision as to costs.'

So it does. And it does so, whether there is a no order for costs rule or not. Mr Mostyn then goes on to describe the *Leadbeater* approach as 'plainly an artifice ... Costs paid do not exist as an asset, and costs outstanding are as much a debt as a debt due to any other creditor.'

**3.44**   But surely this is to overlook the fact that any figure is 'an artifice' in purely philosophical terms? A figure on a page is an abstraction. It represents the only way in which those who prepare calculations – schedules of assets in ancillary relief cases – can represent at a given time an individual's apparent

---

64   And see **2.7** et seq above.

worth. The value of a pension fund represents perhaps the ultimate in the abstractions to which the ancillary relief jurisdiction must resort. It is much more elusive as a figure than is a party's paid costs. Further, it will be recalled that when it comes to valuation of an asset it is conventional – indeed, it must be good practice – to deduct costs of its sale and any anticipated tax which will arise on its sale. These figures are entirely an artifice, but they help to represent the perceived true value of an asset.

**3.45** If this analysis is to be accepted, how can it be any more artificial to credit back costs which have been paid – whether incurred, or paid on account? And, as will be seen, not to credit costs paid to a parties' lawyers back into the asset schedule will directly disadvantage the poorest members of society: by definition the legally aided party will not pay costs to his or her lawyers, and will therefore end up paying half the paying party's costs if the court splits the assets equally.

## Fairness and the *Leadbeater* principle

**3.46** In reality, not to exclude costs must in many cases lead to unfairness; and it inevitably means that the party whose lawyers are less expensive ends up paying for a proportionate amount of the costs of the more expensive lawyers (subject to any conduct costs orders).

*Example 1*

| | |
|---|---:|
| Total net assets (ignoring costs) | 1,000,000 |
| H's costs | (100,000) |
| W's costs | (50,000) |
| Assets net of costs | 850,000 |
| | |
| On a 50:50 split each party has | **425,000** |

Thus W pays her own costs of £50,000 and £25,000 towards H's costs.

*Example 2*

| | |
|---|---:|
| Net assets at the time of hearing | 850,000 |
| H's costs due and costs paid on account | 100,000 |
| W's costs | 50,000 |
| Assets with costs added back | 1,000,000 |

On a 50:50 split, each party has £500,000 from which its own costs have been paid.

*Example 3*

| | |
|---|---:|
| Total net assets (ignoring costs) | 1,000,000 |
| H's costs | (100,000) |
| W's costs | (50,000) |
| Assets net of costs | 850,000 |

W receives 60% of the parties' assets                                         **510,000**

Thus W pays her own costs of £50,000 and £40,000 towards H's costs.

**3.47**     The above calculations show very simply the fairness of crediting back costs. In the first and third examples, the wife pays part of the husband's much higher costs bill if the *Leadbeater* exercise is ignored. Each party can, to some degree, choose how much they spend on the litigation. If the costs are left in the equation before division, then the profligate pays no penalty. If the *Leadbeater* calculation is done – and it is not difficult since all the necessary information, up-to-date, will be available at trial in the parties' Form H1 – there is then no question of the party who chooses the lawyers who are more efficient and cost-effective being penalised because the other party chooses lawyers who are expensive or inefficient.

### *Leadbeater* and legal aid (public funding)

**3.48**     It is where legal aid is available to one party but not the other that any jettisoning of the *Leadbeater* principle becomes most starkly unfair – Mr Mostyn QC only contemplated its demise in 'a big money case, where the assets exceed the aggregate of the parties' needs'.[65] This would exclude almost all legal aid cases, and probably the vast majority of ancillary relief litigation before district judges around the country.

**3.49**     Whether in 'big money' cases, legal aid cases and cases in between, it would seem generally to be unfortunate if any court, when exercising its discretion as to distribution of matrimonial assets, did not credit back into the asset base any amount already paid by either party as costs, whether already incurred or only on account; for not to do so risks one party having to pay the other's costs by the back-door. That, as Wilson J observes, must surely be 'to stand justice on her head'?

---

[65]    Para [92], see n 63 above.

# 4.   CONDUCT, MISCONDUCT AND WASTED COSTS

## INTRODUCTION

### Conduct as an issue in orders for costs

**4.1**    An order for costs in ancillary relief proceedings can only be made where the court decides to depart from the 'general rule'.[1] The court may depart from that general rule in the following circumstances:

- Where it decides to do so specifically in the case of the 'conduct' of the intended paying party and as prescribed by r 2.71(4)(b). It will be in these circumstances that the court most often makes an order for costs in ancillary relief proceedings.

- The court may decide to depart from the general rule and make an order for costs in its discretion.[2]

- The court may make an order based on the 'misconduct' of a party or the party's legal representative.[3]

- Finally, the court may make a wasted costs order.[4]

**4.2**    There are clear legal conceptual associations – degrees of conduct which is disapproved of by the courts to differing extents – which link each of the first, third and fourth of these options. Each implies levels of conduct which carry a costs penalty, whether against a party or the party's legal representative; and in each category of costs order there is a clear reference to whether or not a party or the party's representative has acted unreasonably.[5] The threshold to be passed for an order for costs moves beyond failure in litigation. The court's disapprobation becomes the starting-point. In some ways that sounds logical; but when an advocate reflects that every final hearing has to be approached with an eye to where the other party's conduct may have fallen foul of the court's approval, the new costs landscape becomes less enticing. And when many hearings end in an inquisition of varying degrees of probing and length, judges may regret the new scheme.

---

1    FPR 1991 r 2.71(4)(a).
2    Supreme Court Act 1981, s 51(1); and see **2.7** above.
3    CPR 1998 r 44.14; considered at **4.24** below.
4    Supreme Court Act 1981, s 51(6); considered at **4.26** below.
5    Supreme Court Act 1981, s 51(7)(a) (in the definition of wasted costs); CPR 1998 r 44.14(1)(b) and FPR 1991 r 2.71(5)(c).

## Costs conduct and ancillary relief conduct

**4.3**    The term 'conduct' is a factor in the court's exercise of its discretion in the disposal of ancillary relief proceedings.[6] Conduct in that context features only very rarely indeed in the court's consideration. This concept of 'conduct' is wholly different from the same term applied in the context of a costs order. That said, there will be cases where the court has reflected litigation conduct, or some other aspect of conduct in the proceedings, in its final order. This might, for example, include an inference drawn from a party's non-disclosure of assets. If that happens the court may need to be wary that it does not punish the offending party twice (referred to as 'double jeopardy' below), both in its distribution of the parties' assets (or perceived assets, where inferences are drawn) and in conduct costs.[7]

**4.4**    The subjects of wasted costs orders and misconduct costs orders will be dealt with briefly at the end of this chapter, primarily in order to make as clear as possible the contrast between them and conduct costs orders under r 2.71(4)(b).

# CONDUCT COSTS

## 'In relation to the proceedings'

**4.5**    Orders for costs in ancillary relief proceedings can only be made where each of the following factors applies:

- the court considers it appropriate to make an order because of a party's conduct 'in relation to the proceedings';

- in making such an order the court must have regard to the factors set out in the list in r 2.71(5), which define conduct in an exclusive list; and

- 'at any stage of the proceedings' a conduct costs order can be made (including 'before[8] or during' the proceedings, and at the first directions appointment).[9]

**4.6**    It might be thought that if the 'general rule' prohibition on costs is breached because a conduct issue has overridden the general rule, then the more liberal regime under CPR 1998 r 44.3[10] might come into play. This cannot be the case, since the operation of r 44.3(3) is excluded altogether from ancillary relief proceedings.[11] There cannot therefore be any question of r 44.3(4) or (5)

---

6    Matrimonial Causes Act 1973, s 25(2)(g).
7    See 'double jeopardy' at **4.22** below.
8    And see *Butcher v Wolfe and Wolfe* [1999] 1 FLR 334, CA.
9    FPR 1991 r 2.61D(2)(e).
10   In all circumstances, other than ancillary relief, r 44.3(4) is mandatory when any civil court decides what order it may make on costs.
11   FPR 1991 r 2.71(1).

operating to any extent on costs orders in ancillary relief proceedings. Nor, so far as conduct is concerned, can they be applied by analogy, since r 2.71(5) provides the judge in ancillary relief with its own checklist. (Rule 44.3(4) might be applied *de facto* if Supreme Court Act 1981, s 51(1) applies because the judge decides not to follow the r 2.71(4)(a) general rule;[12] but that will depend on how the individual judge chooses to operate his or her unfettered discretion.)

## Indemnity or standard basis costs

**4.7** It may be appropriate in many instances under r 2.71(4)(b) to seek indemnity costs,[13] though the rule does not give any specific indications on the subject. Indemnity costs are defined by CPR 1998 r 44.4(1), though this rule is silent as to when indemnity costs might be awarded. This may be deliberate. A decision between standard and indemnity costs is entirely a matter for judicial discretion. For similar reasons the Court of Appeal has been reluctant to give guidance on when an indemnity order might be appropriate. Indeed, that court's decisions conflict on whether or not indemnity orders are designed to carry a stigma and to connote court disapproval, or merely to denote that the circumstances justifying an award of costs is outside the norm.

**4.8** What is not in doubt is that there is a clear element amongst the reasons for ordering indemnity costs that a party has been responsible for conduct – short of 'misconduct' – of which the court disapproves. Therefore it would seem appropriate for the court to be clear on what is its attitude to the conduct. There follow examples to illustrate contrasts in forms of conduct which might attract standard, as against indemnity, orders for costs:

(1) There will be actions to which a party or legal representative commits himself or herself which, with the benefit of hindsight – 'if I knew then what I know now'[14] – would not have happened. Such actions might come within 'conduct' in the r 2.71(5) list, though it may not consist of conduct of which the court can or should, in stigmatic terms, disapprove. Costs on the indemnity basis should not normally be awarded.

---

12   See **2.11** above.
13   CPR 1998 r 44.4(1).
14   This is akin to Sir Thomas Bingham's infantryman's defence in *Ridehalgh v Horsefield* [1994] 2 FLR 194 at 209 applied there to the advocate in court; but similar principles apply: 'Any judge who is invited to make or contemplates making an order arising out of an advocate's conduct of court proceedings must make full allowance for the fact that an advocate in court, like a commander in battle, often has to make decisions quickly and under pressure, in the fog of war and ignorant of developments on the other side of the hill. Mistakes will inevitably be made, things done which the outcome shows to have been unwise.'

(2)     Akin to this will be the application pursued or the evidence – perhaps expert evidence – which turns out not to have had the probative or other value which might have been expected. Company valuations are ever a difficult area: if the company is an income stream for both (support of one party and periodical payments for another) its valuation may be unnecessary.[15] Obtaining evidence which is of minimal or no ultimate value may be conduct within r 2.71(5)(c) or (e), but not such as to deserve indemnity basis costs.

(3)     As against this will be the steps taken or the application pursued which, say, have an element of recklessness. This might include insistence on disclosure which comes from an unreasonable or obsessive attitude by one party to their spouse or partner; or, on the other hand, the unhelpful failure to give disclosure or to obstruct other enquiries.

**4.9**     Conduct in the examples given at (1) and (2) – though likely to be regarded as conduct within the terms of r 2.71(5) – is entirely explicable. The type of conduct referred to at (3) (considered further below) is likely to incur the court's disapproval and therefore to merit costs on the indemnity basis. If an order for costs is silent on the basis for assessment, then any costs awarded will be assessed on the standard basis.[16]

## Notice of conduct allegations to be raised

**4.10**     The *President's Practice Direction*[17] proposes that a party 'who intend[s] to seek a costs order against another party in proceedings to which [FPR 1991 r 2.71] applies should ordinarily make this plain in open correspondence or in skeleton arguments before the date of the hearing'. The proposed paying party is on notice that arguments may be raised, necessary defences can be mounted and the court may have an indication of the extent of arguments before the end of the hearing. Any suggestion that conduct costs arguments need to be raised in the course of a hearing should be resisted, though there may be a need for some examination-in-chief or cross-examination of a party on certain conduct points.

## 'Conduct', what 'conduct'?

**4.11**     Rule 2.71(5) sets out an exhaustive list of factors which the court must take into account in defining conduct. The list comprises four which are

---

[15]  See eg *V v V (Financial Relief)* [2005] 2 FLR 697, Coleridge J. In refusing W leave to adduce evidence as to the valuation of his shares, Coleridge J told her that he could value the company adequately himself by reference to *At a Glance* (FLBA, annual publication).

[16]  CPR 1998 r 44.4(4)(a).

[17]  [2006] 1 FLR 864 at para 4 (text in Appendix below).

conduct – by which is meant, in effect, 'misconduct'[18] – and two which are merely factors to weigh in the balance: any 'open offer to settle' and the 'financial effect on the parties of any costs order'.[19] The question of open offers will be considered separately below; and the financial effect of orders is touched on elsewhere.[20] The remaining four factors, it may be noted in passing, are derived from provisions in CPR 1998 r 44.3(5) which, as a source for interpretation, may prove helpful.

**4.12** As already mentioned, part of the impetus for the new rules came from the *cri de coeur* of Mr Nicholas Mostyn QC who, when sitting in the Family Division as a Deputy High Court judge, was confronted with rules which he and Mr Lewis Marks QC found 'incomprehensible'.[21] In the case in question, Mr Mostyn speculated on the subject of ancillary relief costs generally and in anticipation of the 'no order' rule. He then went on to the question of conduct costs as follows:

> '**[92]** [The] starting point [of no order for costs] should be readily departed from where unreasonableness by one or other party is demonstrated.
>
> **[94]** Unreasonableness may encompass the following:
>
> > (1) failure to give full and frank disclosure;
> > (2) other culpable conduct of the litigation such as the unreasonable and unsuccessful pursuit of a particular issue or other meritless tactical posturing;
> > (3) the failure to negotiate or the adoption of a manifestly unreasonable stance in the *Calderbank* correspondence.
>
> **[95]** This is not intended to be an exhaustive list. There may be other instances of unreasonableness …
>
> **[97]** Nor should anything I have said be interpreted as diluting the positive duty to negotiate. This duty is enunciated by *Gojkovic v Gojkovic and Another* and by *A v A (Costs Appeal)* [1996] 1 FLR 14 where Singer J said at 25:
>
> > "The lesson of this case, which litigants and lawyers alike must recognise and give effect to, is that just because ancillary relief applications have to be conducted and prepared in the fraught emotional atmosphere that so often and understandably exists after marriage and its breakdown, nevertheless that does not mean that common sense and commercial realities can be allowed to fly out of the window. A spouse who does not respond constructively to a *Calderbank* offer, whether a good offer as in this case or only one that is bad or indifferent, stymies whatever chance there is of settlement. Such a spouse cannot with impunity expect immunity from responsibility for that …"

---

18 Good conduct is not unheard of, even in matrimonial litigation. 'Misconduct' is also a term of art in the costs jurisdiction: see **4.24** below.
19 FPR 1991 r 2.71(5)(b) and (e).
20 See **3.35** above.
21 *GW v MW* [2003] 2 FLR 108, see **1.15** above.

I agree with every word of this passage. The husband's conduct in that case can be characterised as manifestly unreasonable. The FDR procedure requires the parties to "use their best endeavours to reach agreement on the matters in issue between them" (FPR 2.61E(6)). I believe that this obligation extends outwith the ambit of the FDR. If a party refuses to negotiate in *Calderbank* correspondence, or adopts a manifestly unreasonable stance, then he or she can expect to be penalised in costs.

[98] Similarly, nothing I say should be taken as giving any encouragement to a party to misbehave in the litigation safe in the knowledge that the starting point will be no order as to costs. The court should be astute to discern meritless tactical posturing, such as filibustering, exorbitant demands for disclosure, or the taking of obviously bad points. When such conduct is demonstrated, it will be characterised as unreasonable and the delinquent party can expect to be penalised in costs. I would hope, however, that at the first appointment, the directions phase of the FDR, or the pre-trial review, the court will be able to identify any such incipient unreasonable conduct and quash it.'

**4.13**    The words of the last paragraph might be taken as a text for what follows, especially in relation to raising or pursuing particular issues. And, in particular, Mr Mostyn alludes helpfully (at [98]) to the important influence on costs of case management.[22] That is not to say that the lawyer can excuse his or her excesses and costs conduct on a failure of case management; but a case which is well managed by the court is likely to give fewer hostages to fortune than a conduct costs inquisition.

### Failure to comply with rules, court orders and practice directions

**4.14**    Terminology very similar to r 2.71(5)(a) – the failure of a party to comply with Family Proceedings Rules (FPR) 1991, any court order or a 'practice direction which the court considers relevant' – occurs in Civil Procedure Rules (CPR) 1998 rr 3.8 and 3.9 which both deal with a 'rule, practice direction or court order'. In particular, CPR 1998 r 3.9 may be of assistance to the intended paying party – that is, the respondent to an application for costs under this provision. Rule 3.9(1) sets out a checklist of factors for the court to take into consideration to provide 'relief from sanctions' which may have been imposed for failure to comply with rules, court orders and practice directions. For example, considerations under r 3.9(1) include whether the failure was intentional, whether there is a good explanation, and whether that failure was caused by the party or his or her legal representative. If for 'relief from sanctions' there is substituted relief from a costs order in the case of r 2.71(5)(a) the list in CPR 1998 r 3.9(1) may prove helpful.

**4.15**    This sub-rule brings into FPR 1991 the term 'practice direction'.[23] It is not defined in FPR 1991; nor is it clear here whether it is intended to be a portmanteau term for the miscellany of practice notes, President's directions, guidance and protocols which the family practitioner now confronts; or whether it applies only to those actually described as 'practice direction'. (In

---

22    Case management and costs is considered in Chapter 6.
23    See the discussion of the variety of concepts which may be comprised in the term 'practice direction' at **2.44** above.

this section and for the present, it will be assumed that the term 'practice direction' is intended to cover most of these directional documents.) The role of the practice direction in CPR 1998 is well defined, Part by Part; and the subservience of the practice direction to the rules is clear.[24] The subservience of the practice direction in family proceedings to statute and to rules is also more or less accepted (subject to the directional document actually representing statute law or delegated legislation correctly).

### Raising and pursuing a 'particular allegation or issue'

**4.16**   Rule 2.71(5)(c) and (d) are taken almost word-for-word from CPR 1991 r 44.3(5)(b) and (c). The conduct raised here consists of two aspects of the taking of points or pursuing issues in litigation:

- was it in the opinion of the court 'reasonable' to raise a particular issue, and then for the applicant to pursue, or the respondent to contest it; and

- a consideration by the court of the means by which a party (a) has pursued or responded to the ancillary relief application or (b) dealt with a particular allegation or issue.

**4.17**   Avoidance of costs under these headings should be perfectly possible for the lawyer who is as clear as possible what are the issues involved in the application before the court.[25] It is then necessary to ensure that the means whereby those issues are pursued comply with the ancillary relief overriding objective and certain other basic guidelines. A party who proceeds in this way should not fall foul of an order under r 2.71(5)(c) or (d).

**4.18**   These basic guidelines are as follows:

(1)   Having defined the issues – of law and of fact – as early as possible, keep these issues under review all the way to trial.

(2)   Ensure that only evidence which is relevant to one or more of these issues is adduced; and if expert evidence is required, ensure that the appropriate permission[26] is obtained form the court *before* the opinion is sought.

(3)   Ensure that only documents or further information which is relevant to one of these issues is sought, whether by questionnaire or further direction of the court.

---

24   See per Auld LJ in *R (on the application of Mount Cook Land Limited) v Westminster City Council* [2003] EWCA Civ 1346, CA at [67]: 'Practice Directions in general supplement the CPR and are made by the Head of the appropriate Division of the High Court under his or her inherent jurisdiction. They are recognised by the 1997 Act, and, for example in section 5(1) and Schedule 1, paragraphs 3 and 6, may in certain circumstances have the effect of provisions that could otherwise be made by way of CPR (see also CPR 8.1(6)(b)). I use the word "recognised" deliberately, for I doubt whether it is correct to assert as a generality, ... that Practice Directions are made "pursuant" to statute or that they have the same authority as the CPR ... In the case of any conflict between the two, the CPR prevails.'

25   For a consideration of definition of issues for trial see **6.10** below.

26   CPR 1998 r 35.4.

(4)     If in doubt, seek directions from the court concerning the particular issue or proposed investigation: if the court has given directions on the issue or allegation based on realistic information from the party seeking the direction, it will be rare for conduct costs to arise.

(5)     At all times bear in mind the r 2.51B(2) overriding objective, in particular the saving of expense and proportionality.

**4.19**   The types of conduct that might be included under this head are infinite[27] but would include:

- inappropriate or obsessive pursuit of a search order,[28] freezing injunction or application in restraint of disposal;

- failure to disclose documents or information, or to disclose in time, or to do so in accordance with court orders, especially where this has necessitated an adjournment, or has not enabled the court properly to exercise its discretion;

- obsessive or disproportionate pursuit of disclosure[29] by, or seeking of information from, the other spouse or partner.[30]

## Any other relevant aspect of conduct in the proceedings

**4.20**   A reference to 'any other aspect of … conduct in the proceedings' plainly gives the court a very wide canvas on which to sketch in orders for costs. It perhaps exonerates the draftsman of the rules from charges of over-prescriptiveness in the exhaustive list which has been set out in r 2.71(5). For r 2.71(5)(e) provides a head of conduct which is closely akin to 'all the circumstances of the case' insofar as they bear upon 'relevant' conduct 'in the proceedings'.

**4.21**   This head plainly equates with 'litigation conduct' and will be regarded in the same way as costs orders and adjustments of capital to compensate the blameless spouse for the other's litigation conduct before the new rules came into operation.

## Double jeopardy

**4.22**   Especially in the light of what is said in paragraph **4.20** above about 'litigation' conduct, the court may need to be wary of placing a party at risk of a form of double jeopardy: first, where there is an inference as to a party having

---

[27]  And see the comments of Mr Nicholas Mostyn QC sitting as a Deputy High Court judge in *GW v RW (Financial Provision: Departure from Equality)* [2003] 2 FLR 108 especially at [98] (above at **4.12**).

[28]  *Burgess v Burgess* [1996] 2 FLR 34, Hale J was a relatively extreme example of a solicitor who pursued his former wife, a GP, with an *Anton Piller* (search) order where he was probably, in reality, seeking evidence of her perceived infidelity. He was condemned in indemnity costs for this exercise.

[29]  See eg *R v M (Wasted Costs Order)* [1996] 1 FLR 750.

[30]  See, for example, *Hildebrand v Hildebrand* [1992] 1 FLR 244, Waite J.

more assets than disclosed, perhaps where disclosure has been inadequate or very late, and the other party's award is inflated accordingly; or secondly where a party's litigation conduct is reflected in the amount of capital ordered to be transferred or paid to them. In either of these instances a party may already have been penalised in terms of adjustment of capital for the party's conduct of his or her case. It might be wrong – though not invariably so – also to order costs against the party for, in effect, the same conduct.

### Whose conduct is it?

**4.23** There are instances where the conduct is not that of the client but of the legal representative, over whom the client has no – or only limited – control. A simple example might be where an adjournment is requested solely for the convenience of the representative. It would be quite wrong to penalise the client here: to assume that the client would pass on to the lawyer any costs order. The costs order – if any can be made – should be as wasted costs or misconduct. It may not be easy for the court to bring the order within the grounds set out in the relevant provisions;[31] but if it is the conduct of the lawyer of a client who is blameless, which has led to costs being thrown away, then the client should not be penalised.

## COSTS IN RELATION TO MISCONDUCT

**4.24** The term 'misconduct' has a particular meaning in the costs jurisdiction,[32] and it must be distinguished from the separate 'wasted costs' jurisdiction.[33] CPR 1998 r 44.14 enables the court, at the time of assessment of costs (whether detailed assessment or summary assessment)[34] to disallow part or all of a party's own legal representative's costs; or to order a party or a party's legal representative to pay another party's legal representatives costs 'which he has caused any other party to incur'. The order can be made on application by the party affected by the misconduct, or by the court on its own initiative. The basis for making the order is that costs have been incurred as a result of conduct, on the part of a party or legal representative, which 'appears to the court [to be] unreasonable or improper'.[35]

**4.25** The words 'unreasonable or improper' can be seen immediately to be the same as in Supreme Court Act 1981, s 51(7) (considered in the next section); and it is likely that a similar standard as under s 51(7) will be required for an order under r 44.14 as for a wasted costs order. The difference between the orders is the time at which they arise: the 'misconduct' order arises where an assessment is under way; whereas a wasted costs order goes wider and application can be made at any time in proceedings and regardless of whether there is an assessment being carried out.

---

31 See **4.24** and **4.26** below.
32 CPR 1998 r 44.14.
33 Supreme Court Act 1981, s 51(7); and see **4.26** below.
34 Given the brief – ie summary – disposal of a summary assessment it is difficult to imagine when a misconduct order might occur other than on detailed assessment.
35 CPR 1998 r 44.14(1)(b).

# WASTED COSTS ORDERS

## Jurisdiction

**4.26** The wasted costs jurisdiction arises from Supreme Court Act 1981, s 51(6), which enables the court to 'disallow, or (as the case may be) order the legal or other representative concerned to meet, the whole of any wasted costs or such part of them as may be determined in accordance with rules of court'. CPR 1998 r 48.7 provides the rule which governs procedure for an order. Any order will be against the legal representative of a party, and an order can only be made where the court takes the view that there has been an 'improper, negligent or unreasonable' act by a legal representative. The court must give the representative notice of its intention to impose this sanction upon a legal representative.

**4.27** The wasted costs jurisdiction was considered authoritatively in *Ridehalgh v Horsefield, and Watson v Watson (Wasted Costs Order)*.[36] In that case the Court of Appeal pointed out that in operation of the jurisdiction, the court must balance two, often conflicting, questions of public interest. On the one hand, lawyers should not be deterred from pursuing their clients' interests for fear of incurring personal liability for costs. On the other hand, litigants need to be protected from financial prejudice caused by any unjustifiable conduct of lawyers. The jurisdiction is one which is entirely discretionary.[37]

## 'Improper, unreasonable or negligent'

**4.28** Supreme Court Act 1981, s 51(7) defines 'wasted costs' as 'any costs incurred by a party ... as a result of any improper, unreasonable or negligent act or omission on the part of any legal or other representative[38] or any employee of such a representative'. These words were considered fully in *Ridehalgh v Horsefield* (above). The Court of Appeal stressed the importance of bringing any application – or threat of an application – within the headings of behaviour by a legal representative set out in s 51(7). It considered each term in s 51(7) as follows:

> (1)    *Improper* – This word covers conduct which might lead to disbarment, striking off or other serious professional penalty. It is not restricted to this and might include other conduct stigmatised by the court in appropriate circumstances.

---

36  [1994] 2 FLR 194.

37  'Just because an application [in this case, to discharge a care order] is plainly doomed to failure it is not necessarily an improper application for a solicitor to advise a party to proceed with' (*Re O (A Minor) (Wasted Costs Application)* [1994] 2 FLR 842 per Connell J at 846H: no wasted costs order).

38  'Legal representative' is defined by Supreme Court Act 1981, s 51(13) as 'legal or other representative' as 'in relation to a party to proceedings, any person exercising a right of audience or right to conduct litigation on his behalf'.

(2)     *Unreasonable* – This term includes conduct which is vexatious or harasses other parties, but it does not include an approach which merely leads to an unsuccessful result or which a more cautious representative might not have adopted.

(3)     *Negligent* – Essentially, this term is to be approached in a non-technical way – ie it is not the same as the tort of negligence. A legal representative may come within the definition by failing to act with the competence reasonably to be expected of a member of the legal profession.

**4.29**    A legal representative is not to be regarded as acting improperly, unreasonably or negligently where pursuing a hopeless case for the client, providing this does not represent an abuse of the court's process. It is the responsibility of a lawyer to present the case and of the court to judge it; but if, for example, solicitors persist in seeking extensive disclosure, they might risk a wasted costs order.[39]

---

[39]   *R v M (Wasted Costs Order)* [1996] 1 FLR 750.

# 5. WITHOUT PREJUDICE PRIVILEGE

## INTRODUCTION

### Privilege defined

**5.1**    A document or other evidence is said to be privileged when a party is permitted to refuse to place before the court otherwise admissible evidence. In this instance the privilege will be that of the person entitled to rely upon it: in the case of legal professional privilege, for example, the privilege belongs to the client (not to his or her lawyer). Thus only the client can waive that privilege, or the client's lawyer on the client's behalf.

**5.2**    Where the term privilege is used in the context of correspondence marked 'without prejudice' or where privilege arises, *de facto*, where parties negotiate with a view to settlement, it is used to denote a completely different form of privilege. What it has in common with legal professional privilege is only that documents or the content of negotiations arising in this way are privileged from disclosure in any existing or subsequent litigation connected with the subject of the correspondence or negotiations.[1] The privilege is that of two people which arises from a quasi-contractual arrangement between them. It follows that 'without prejudice' privilege cannot be waived by only one party.[2] The justification for the privilege is that it is public policy to encourage people to negotiate their differences rather than litigate them to the end through the courts; and it is thought that litigants will negotiate more freely if they can do so without their negotiation being part of the evidence in any ensuing trial.[3]

**5.3**    By seeking to render the *Calderbank* letter inadmissible the new ancillary relief costs rules appear to intend that all negotiations be 'open'. This may overlook the fact that it is the act of negotiating which creates the privilege, not that the words 'without prejudice' are used. The concept of the 'open offer to settle' is embedded in the rules and for ancillary relief alone no other offer will be admissible at all, or on the issue of costs. It will be interesting to see how this term – set against existing legal principle on what defines the adherence of privilege to a document or negotiations – will be regarded by those entrusted with interpretation of the new law.

---

1    *Rush & Tomkins Ltd v Greater London Council* [1989] AC 1280.
2    *Cutts v Head* (below); and see eg *Le Foe v Le Foe and Woolwich* [2001] 2 FLR 970, Nicholas Mostyn QC, sitting as a Deputy High Court judge.
3    See eg *Cutts v Head* [1984] Ch 290, [1984] 1 All ER 597, CA.

# OPEN OFFERS

## Offers which are not open

**5.4**    No offer to settle which is not open shall be admissible,[4] save at the FDR (where 'offers, proposals or responses made wholly or partly without prejudice' must be filed at court and, for the FDR appointment are admissible).[5] This rule seeks to overturn the long-established effects of *Calderbank v Calderbank*.[6] If the new rules prove to extend also to appeals, alongside the no costs order rule, it will undoubtedly ensure that many more cases go to trial and probably on to appeal. The *Calderbank* teeth have been pulled.

**5.5**    The term 'open offer' is not defined. It is presumably intended to include an open proposal, a counter-offer and an open acceptance; though the same set of rules at one point stresses the different terms 'offers, proposals or responses' (Family Proceedings Rules (FPR) 1991 r 2.61E(3), in respect of the FDR). If they are distinguished there, are we supposed to assume that the different concepts have been conflated (as they are in Civil Procedure Rules (CPR) 1998) when it comes to costs?

**5.6**    The point may prove of significance, in the sense that it is only a person who has something to part with who can offer it for transfer or settlement of a claim for lump sum or periodical payments. A party who is in the position of claimant – for example, the party who has no pension and, for the present, is no longer living in the house – might be said to be incapable of making an offer. That party can only put forward a proposal to settle. If that is marked 'without prejudice', is it admissible on the subject of costs since it is 'not an open *offer* to settle': it is a *Calderbank* proposal. The point may not see the light of day, but it is disappointing that it was not dealt with more clearly – or indeed at all - in the drafting of the rules.[7]

**5.7**    'Without prejudice' privilege does not go with these new rules. Parties can still choose to negotiate on terms that are privileged from disclosure to the court. However, the new ancillary relief costs regime cuts across the *Calderbank* effect of such correspondence.

## Negotiations for settlement

**5.8**    As already mentioned, it is the existence of negotiations between the parties that attracts the privilege,[8] not the fact that a party writes 'without prejudice' on the letter. There may prove to be an appreciable number of parties who think they have written an open letter merely by omitting the words 'without prejudice' on a letter. That does not, of itself, make the letter 'an open

---

4    FPR 1991 r 2.71(6).
5    FPR 1991 r 2.61E(3) and (4).
6    [1976] Fam 93, (1975) FLR Rep 113, CA.
7    A failure to align r 2.61E(3) with r 2.71(6).
8    See **5.3** above.

offer to settle' (in the terms of the rule). The writer of a letter in negotiations which is intended to be open should use a form of words in every letter which makes it clear that each individual letter is intended to be open, for example:

> 'Though part of negotiations, this letter is intended to be open within the terms of Family Proceedings Rules 1991 r 2.71(6).'

**5.9**    Further, without prejudice privilege is joint and cannot be waived unilaterally. It is probable that there will be some very unusual negotiations where one party prefers to negotiate on terms which are covered by 'without prejudice' privilege, whilst the other party wants his or her side of the correspondence to be open. The open correspondence cannot refer to the correspondence to which privilege attaches. The privileged correspondence can refer to the open letters.

**5.10**    Where an offer or proposal for settlement is accepted and the correspondence or oral terms can be said to comprise an agreement, then the privilege goes and the document or the content of the negotiations is admissible by either party as part of their evidence.[9] Insofar as hitherto privileged correspondence is not 'open', but is now opened by the agreement, does it become open, or does its 'not-openness' blight it for all times in terms of r 2.71(6)? These are not matters of discretion. They are matters of law and of interpretation of delegated legislation. The rule-maker's failure to anticipate this will need to await judicial interpretation.

# *CALDERBANK* AND CIVIL PROCEDURE RULES 1998 PART 36

## The origins of the *Calderbank* letter

**5.11**    It has long been the law that a defendant could protect himself or herself from an adverse costs order by paying money into court. If the court awarded the plaintiff in the action less than the money paid in, that plaintiff might expect to pay the defendant's costs (as well as his or her own) from at or shortly after the date of payment in. The impecunious defendant could not protect himself or herself in this way; nor could the litigant involved in property or matrimonial proceedings.

**5.12**    In *Calderbank v Calderbank*[10] Cairns LJ proposed a scheme, to which the case gave its name, which enabled a party to ancillary relief proceedings to make an offer 'without prejudice', but on terms that he or she could unilaterally waive privilege when any costs came to be applied for. On the wife's application for costs in *Calderbank* and her request to place before the court an offer letter written without prejudice, he held as follows:

> 'There are various other types of proceedings well known to the court where protection has been able to be afforded to a party who wants to

---

9    *Walker v Wilsher* (1889) 23 QBD 335, CA.
10    (1975) FLR Rep 123, CA.

make a compromise of that kind and where payment-in is not an appropriate method. One is in proceedings before the Lands Tribunal where the amount of compensation is in issue and where the method that is adopted is that of a sealed offer which is not made without prejudice but which remains concealed from the tribunal until the decision on the substantive issue has been made and the offer is then opened when the discussion as to costs takes place. Another example is in the Admiralty Division where there is commonly a dispute between the owners of two vessels that have been in collision as to the apportionment of blame between them. It is common practice for an offer to be made by one party to another of a certain apportionment. If that is not accepted no reference is made to that offer in the course of the hearing until it comes to costs, and then if the court's apportionment is as favourable to the party who made the offer as what was offered, or more favourable to him, then costs will be awarded on the same basis as if there had been a payment in.

I see no reason why some similar practice should not be adopted in relation to such matrimonial proceedings in relation to finances as we have been concerned with.

Mr Millar drew our attention to a provision in the Matrimonial Causes Rules 1968 with reference to damages which were then payable by a correspondent, provision to the effect that an offer might be made in the form that it was without prejudice to the issue as to damages but reserving the right of the co-respondent to refer to it on the issue of costs. It appears to me that it would be equally appropriate that it should be permissible to make an offer of that kind in such proceedings as we have been dealing with and I think that that would be an appropriate way in which a party who was willing to make a compromise could put it forward. I do not consider that any amendment of the Rules of the Supreme Court is necessary to enable this to be done.'

## Civil Procedure Rules 1998 Part 36

**5.13**    The *Calderbank* letter and its direct descendant, the Part 36 offer, survive in other jurisdictions, as indeed they do in all other family proceedings – Children Act 1989, Sch 1; Trust of Land and Appointment of Trustees Act 1996 etc. The without prejudice letter still survives in the ancillary relief jurisdiction. It remains privileged. It may remain a potent tool to assist negotiations; and of course the FDR itself, with any *Calderbank* correspondence required to be filed, remains behind the veil of privilege. However, such correspondence and any negotiations cannot be referred to on the question of costs. What is described in the rules as 'an open offer to settle' is the only form of offer to settle which is admissible.[11] Feigned blindness will afflict the family judge when both parties urge him or her to look at correspondence in respect of which they have both waived their joint privilege.

---

[11]    FPR 1991 r 2.71(6).

# 6.   PROPORTIONALITY AND RELEVANCE

## INTRODUCTION

### Overriding objective

**6.1**    The purpose of this chapter is to look at various aspects of the existing ancillary relief rules in the context of costs and of 'saving expense',[1] and in the context of possible conduct costs.[2] Justice and fairness are not necessarily achieved by cutting costs, but nor is there any guarantee of fairness because as much money as possible is spent on a piece of litigation. By the same token, tight time limits and a rush to trial may deliver marginal costs savings, but in such a climate fairness is by no means guaranteed. Plainly unwarranted delay in proceedings is likely to increase costs.

**6.2**    The ancillary relief jurisdiction is unique, so far, amongst the family proceedings covered by the Family Proceedings Rules (FPR) 1991 in having its own overriding objective. Mostly this is taken from Civil Procedure Rules (CPR) 1998.[3] Courts have a duty, says FPR 1991 r 2.51B, to further the overriding objective by 'actively managing cases'.[4] Active case management, continues the rule, includes a number of components, the most important of which, for present purposes, are:

- identifying the issues at an early date[5] (and, it will be suggested here, keeping the issues under review);

- regulating the extent of disclosure and expert evidence so that they are proportionate to the issues;[6]

- fixing timetables, giving directions and otherwise efficiently controlling the progress of a case.[7]

---

1    FPR 1991 r 2.51B(2)(b): part of the ancillary relief rules overriding objective.
2    FPR 1991 r 2.71(4)(b).
3    CPR 1998 Parts 1 and 3.
4    FPR 1991 r 2.51B(5).
5    FPR 1991 r 2.51B(6)(c).
6    FPR 1991 r 2.51B(6)(d).
7    FPR 1991 r 2.51B(6)(e) and (h).

## Proportionality: 'saving expense'

**6.3**     It may be thought to be a statement of the obvious, but if the requirements of case management were observed fully by the parties, their advisers and the courts then the cost of ancillary relief litigation would be contained; and probably the incidence of costs would fall appreciably. Further, if parties prepare their cases with the overriding objective permanently in mind, conduct costs orders[8] must surely be rare? And, so the argument goes, central to case management is a clear assessment of the issues for trial, which assessment must be kept under review throughout the process up to final hearing.

**6.4**     What follows, therefore, will be as much about saving expense as about the new costs rules; but in a jurisdiction where costs are now to become almost entirely dependent on proof of a litigant's default – or at least some form of behaviour of which the court, however mildly, disapproves – case management and saving expense must, to a large degree, go hand-in-hand with avoiding conduct costs orders.

# DEFINING THE ISSUES: RELEVANCE AND ADMISSIBILITY

## Evidence and procedure

**6.5**     Without a set of facts (otherwise evidence – even though part or all of that evidence is agreed) there can be no trial. Procedure is the means whereby, according to the appropriate law and procedural rules, evidence relevant to the issues to be tried comes before the court. For example, disclosure is a rule of evidence. Primary legislation provides – at least impliedly – that full disclosure must be provided to the court in ancillary relief proceedings.[9] Procedure defines when and by what means relevant disclosure is to be given to the court and to other parties.

## Relevance and admissibility

**6.6**     Central to the rules of evidence is the requirement that only evidence which is relevant, or sufficiently relevant, to the issues before the court is admissible. Thus to determine what evidence is to be before the court it is necessary to define the issues for trial. In a jurisdiction which is heavily dependant on the exercise of judicial discretion, this may prove more difficult than in a jurisdiction which is more dependent on the law for its disposal: one judge may regard as relevant to the exercise of his or her discretion completely different matters to another judge, who it was that gave directions for trial of the application.[10] Until the ancillary relief jurisdiction can provide the same

---

8     FPR 1991 r 2.71(4)(b); and see Chapter 4.
9     Matrimonial Causes Act 1973, s 25(1) as explained in *Livesey v Jenkins* [1985] AC 424, [1985] 1 All ER 106, [1985] 2 WLR 47, [1985] FLR 813.
10    For example, one judge might refuse leave to adduce certain expert evidence; where at trial the judge might want to rely on (say) valuation of a party's shares in his company.

judge to deal with pre-trial case management issues and the trial of the application itself, this problem will persist.

## Categorisation of issues

**6.7** A definition of issues in the case, then, is the essence of preparation for trial, and of case management of the process leading to trial. Case management will be the means whereby the court ensures proportionality and an economic disposal of the application based upon all the evidence relevant to those issues. Definition of the issues should therefore, wherever possible, be a co-operative exercise between the parties or their lawyers and the judge.

**6.8** From the point of view of costs – and for avoidance of a conduct costs order – an analysis of the issues in a case is fundamental:

(1) It enables the lawyer preparing the trial to eliminate unnecessary evidence and information. In evidential terms, evidence is not adduced which is not relevant. The client is thereby saved needless costs.

(2) In a jurisdiction – that of ancillary relief costs – which is now based on 'conduct', it is plainly important for the lawyer to identify which issues and allegations are relevant to protect his or her own client; and to identify which are less than relevant to identify whether it is reasonable for a party 'to raise, pursue or contest' that particular issue.[11]

**6.9** In what follows, issues will be categorised as follows:

- *primary issues* – an issue on which the court will be requested to, and can, make an order[12] – as set out in Matrimonial Causes Act 1973;

- *issues of law*; and

- *evidential issues* – that is, issues of fact or of opinion (expert evidence).

## ISSUES IN THE ANCILLARY RELIEF JURISDICTION

### Issues in disposal of the application

**6.10** The categorisation adopted here assumes that the object of the application from either party's point of view is to secure from the court a disposal of their ancillary relief claims; and that that disposal can only be based upon the menu of orders available under Matrimonial Causes Act 1973, Part II.

---

11 FPR 1991 r 2.71(5)(c); and see **4.5** above.
12 Note: the reminder in *Dinch v Dinch* [1987] 2 FLR 162, [1987] 1 WLR 252, HL – that the court can only make orders, as distinct from taking undertakings – in accordance with their powers under Matrimonial Causes Act 1973.

These issues are dealt with by the court entirely in the exercise of its discretion. They are described here as 'primary issues'. The secondary issues – namely issues of law and evidential issues – represent matters on which the court must make findings to deal with the primary issues. They will therefore rarely be matters of judicial discretion.

**6.11**    By definition, something that is agreed is not an issue; and, as such, it may be incorporated 'by consent' into the order or made the subject of an agreement (or 'undertakings') as a pre-amble to the order.

**6.12**    Certain secondary issues may usefully be tried as preliminary – that is, as quite separate – issues.[13] The possible saving of expense will be an important factor in the whether the court is willing to release an issue for separate trial, for if no costs can be seen as being likely to be saved it will rarely be advantageous to separate off an issue for separate hearing.

## Issues of law

**6.13**    With evidential issues, issues of law must be decided by the court before a final order – disposal of a primary issue – can be made. Pure issues of law arise only relatively infrequently in ancillary relief proceedings. When they occur they may be appropriate to be tried as a separate issue;[14] and this will be the more so if a third party is involved.[15] Mixed issues of law and of fact arise, say, where the parties appear to have arrived at an agreement in correspondence,[16] but where one seeks to say there is no agreement. This can be illustrated by the following example.

### *Illustration: the 'agreement' issue*

**6.14**    H has apparently agreed in correspondence to a settlement of financial issues. A consent order embodying the terms of what was thought to have been agreed. H refuses to assent to this.[17] Even if there is held to have been an agreement, the primary issues remain to be tried; but the agreement (if it was one) is only likely to be overturned if there are 'special circumstances' why it should be.[18] The issues for determination at this preliminary stage are:

- *Was there an agreement?* – This is a matter of **law** to be determined from the correspondence.[19] Derived from the correspondence it will be a matter of contract law whether there was an agreement. (The fact that if there is

---

13    See **6.21** below.
14    See eg *T v T (Judicial Separation)* (2000) Fam Law case summaries, July 517, where it was held that an earlier judicial separation consent order which dealt with capital, did not prevent a party returning to court to try again ancillary relief issues as a whole on a subsequent divorce.
15    *TL v ML and others (Ancillary Relief: Claims against Assets of Extended Family)* [2005] EWHC 2860 (Fam), [2006] 1 FLR 864, Nicholas Mostyn QC sitting as a Deputy High Court judge.
16    *Walker v Wilsher* (1889) 23 QBD 335, CA; and see **5.21** above.
17    For a recent example of this type of issue see *A v B (Financial Relief; Agreements)* [2005] EWHC 314 (Fam), [2005] 2 FLR 730, Black J.
18    *Edgar v Edgar* (1981) 2 FLR 19, CA; and see *Xydhias v Xydhias* [1999] 1 FLR 683, CA.
19    It is possible to conceive of a case where the agreement may be evidenced partly or entirely from discussions between the parties. Whether or not there was an agreement will then turn first on the facts, and only then on law.

an agreement, then any privilege attaching to the correspondence goes,[20] is a matter of law also; but it follows from a finding on this first issue and is not therefore a separate head).

- *Was the objecting party independently advised?* – This is a matter of **fact**.

- *Was that advice 'bad legal advice?'*[21] – This is a matter of mixed **law and fact**.

- *Was the objecting party put under 'undue pressure'?* – Though this is essentially a legal term, adjudication upon the issue it raises is a matter of **fact**.

**6.15** If an agreement is established, it then becomes one of the factors to be taken into consideration under s 25(2) (whether as 'conduct' or as part of 'all the circumstances').[22] It will be a matter of judicial discretion as to the extent it is taken into account; though that discretion will be guided by indications given by the Court of Appeal in such cases as *Edgar*.

## Evidential issues

**6.16** Evidential issues arise where matters of fact or of opinion ('expert evidence') arise. As with issues of law, the judge must make findings upon any evidential issues before the court can proceed to exercise its discretion and dispose of the primary issue.

**6.17** For the lawyer preparing the case, this is the area that is most critical, both in terms of expense and for a successful outcome. If the appropriate relevant evidence is called, the court is in a position to make suitable findings. If the evidence is not available to the court, the desired outcome for the client may not be achievable. If evidence which is not relevant is called, the client may pay unnecessary costs; and it will a short step to a finding that 'a particular allegation or issue' has been pursued in such a 'manner' that conduct costs follow.[23]

**6.18** *Piglowska v Piglowski*[24] provides a dramatic example of costs expended on a case essentially involving judicial discretion; but, for present purposes, involving a failure to marshall all necessary evidence. The husband wanted to move back from Poland to the South London area where he had lived with his former wife. To do this he wanted the parties' former matrimonial home to be sold and the wife to re-house herself. The district judge made an order which enabled the wife to stay in the home. The judge, on appeal, refused to admit, on the husband's application, further evidence as to how the wife might re-house herself, and refused the husband's appeal. On giving leave to appeal, the Court of Appeal refused to admit the further evidence, but assumed that the wife

---

20  See **5.10** above.
21  *Edgar v Edgar* (above); further explained in *Camm v Camm* (1983) 4 FLR 577, CA.
22  See eg *A v B (Financial Relief; Agreements)* (above) at [32].
23  FPR 1991 r 2.71(5)(d).
24  [1999] 2 FLR 763 HL.

could re-house herself satisfactorily if a sale were ordered. In the House of Lords, Lord Hoffman expressed the following opinion:[25]

> '... [T]he Court of Appeal were in effect taking judicial notice of prices in the south-east London property market. In *Martin (BH) v Martin (D)* [1978] Fam 12, 20G–H, (1977) FLR Rep 444, 450E, Ormrod LJ cautioned against this free-wheeling approach to judicial notice:
>
>> "... whenever it is to be argued that the wife could find alternative accommodation for herself out of her share of the equity, whatever that may be ... there should be evidence put before the court to that effect. The unsupported assertions and speculations which are made in the course of argument in these cases are not satisfactory. It means the court has to use its own imprecise knowledge of the property market and may well make mistakes. So if it is going to be said that the wife could get alternative accommodation, let there be some evidence to that effect. Otherwise it will have to be assumed that it is not possible."
>
> Obviously there will be cases where the margin of error is wide enough to allow judicial notice to be taken. But in this case there was no such margin.'

**6.19**    On the costs implications of the process of appeals in the *Piglowska* case, Lord Hoffman famously concluded his speech as follows:[26]

> '[Finally], there is the principle of proportionality between the amount at stake and the legal resources of the parties and the community which it is appropriate to spend on resolving the dispute. In a case such as the present, the legal system provides for the possibility of three successive appeals from the decision at first instance. The first is as of right and the second and third are subject to screening processes which themselves may involve more than one stage. If one includes applications for leave, the facts of this case, by the time it reached the Court of Appeal, had been considered by five differently constituted tribunals. This cannot be right. To allow successive appeals in the hope of producing an answer which accords with perfect justice is to kill the parties with kindness. [He then considered what has become Access to Justice Act 1999, s 55.]
>
> This provision, if enacted, would have prevented the further appeal in this case ... I would only add that even if a case does raise an important point of practice or principle, the Court of Appeal should consider carefully whether it is fair to have it decided at the expense of parties with very limited resources or whether it should wait for a more suitable vehicle.'

---

[25]    Ibid at 782.
[26]    Ibid at 785.

## Primary issue

**6.20**   A primary issue is one on which the court will be requested to, and can, make an order. In the present context, resolution of the primary issue will arise as an issue on costs in such of the following circumstances where:

(1) An issue – for example transfer of shares in a private company or a pension sharing order – is pursued in a way which is obsessive or where, to the objective observer, it might be said to be hopeless.

(2) An issue is pursued but is rejected out of hand by the court and in circumstances where a favourable result for the applicant, on the particular issue, was unlikely.

# TRIAL OF A SEPARATE ISSUE

## Case management and Family Proceedings Rules 1991

**6.21**   CPR 1998 r 1.4(2)(b) and (d) provides that 'active case management' includes 'identifying the issues at an early stage' and 'deciding the order in which issues are to be resolved'. The regime introduced by CPR 1998 encourages the courts to split issues for separate trial where this would be appropriate, and especially where this might have a costs saving consequence. FPR 1991 r 2.51B(6)(c) ('identifying the issues at an early stage') is in similar terms to CPR 1998 r 1.4(2) and has a similar effect for ancillary relief proceedings. If used appropriately the costs-saving consequences of this provision are difficult to exaggerate.

## When to order a separate trial

**6.22**   A criterion for deciding whether or not to split off an issue for separate trial might be: will a decision on the preliminary issue help to settle the case and thereby save costs?[27] The only clear justification for separating issues on points which are unresolved as between the parties will be the saving of costs (different questions arise where third parties are involved).[28] Thus a preliminary hearing might be ordered:

(1) Where to resolve the preliminary point might help to settle the application because without an answer on that point it is impossible for the parties to define the total value of their assets: thus valuation of a particular asset, of shares, of a pension fund, with competing opinion evidence called, could be tried separately.

---

[27]   See FPR 1991 r 2.51B(6)(b): active case management includes encouragement to the parties to settle their differences through mediation. Mediation is difficult where there is an unresolved issue about, say, valuation of an asset of substance.

[28]   See **6.23** below.

(2) In the case of disputed ownership of particular assets as between one party and a third party, the question of ownership must be tried separately[29] (this would include issues in connection with the insolvency of one party).

(3) Where there are trust issues which involve third parties, including members of one or other parties' family, cohabitants and so on, these must be tried separately.

(4) To deal with unanswered questions as to income or resources or as to beneficial ownership by one or other party of other defined assets.[30]

## Issues involving third parties

**6.23** In *TL v ML and others (Ancillary Relief: Claims against Assets of Extended Family)*[31] one of the issues which the court was called upon to consider was the ownership of a property – referred to there only as 24AL, a spacious mansion flat in St John's Wood – legal title to which was vested in the husband's brother, but which the wife asserted belonged beneficially to the husband. The case came before Mr Mostyn QC as a final hearing with the husband and wife and the husband's brother and their father, all as parties and represented.

**6.24** Mr Mostyn QC dealt first with the issue over the beneficial ownership of 24AL. The wife had claimed that the husband was entitled to it under a trust of land; so, said Mr Mostyn QC, the legal owner should be joined, directions be given for the issue to be fully pleaded – so the claim can be 'approached on exactly the same basis as if it were being determined in the Chancery Division'.[32] The claim should then 'be heard separately as a preliminary issue' so that the parties then know 'at an early stage whether or not the property in question falls within the dispositive powers of the court'. A meaningful FDR can then take place and the expensive attendance of the third party at the final hearing can be avoided.

## Implied trusts

**6.25** Where a third party alleges a beneficial interest in a property, legal title to which is held by one or other or both of the parties, then unquestionably the points on case management and trial of a preliminary issue proposed in *TL v ML* arise. For example, where one party's parents provide cash for the parties' purchase of their matrimonial home, then that cash may be a gift, it may be a loan; but, depending on the circumstances, it may give rise to a resulting trust. The legal owners – husband and wife – hold on trust for themselves and the parents who have a beneficial entitlement based on their investment into the purchase of the property. If the (now former) matrimonial home is subject to a

---

29 *TL v ML and others (Ancillary Relief: Claims against Assets of Extended Family)* above.
30 See *OS v DS*; and note availability of *Khanna* hearing to call for documents at a hearing preliminary to the trial.
31 [2005] EWHC 2860 (Fam), [2006] 1 FLR 864, Nicholas Mostyn QC sitting as a Deputy High Court judge [34]–[37].
32 At [34] and [36].

resulting trust that plainly affects the value of the total assets available for distribution. The question must be resolved before final hearing.

**6.26**   An issue such as this can be pleaded under Trust of Land and Appointment of Trustees Act 1996, s 14.[33] It can be pleaded by any of the parties and the s 14 issue can be tried separately on a set of pleadings: either framed following directions in the ancillary relief application, as recommended by Mr Mostyn QC, or within parallel CPR 1998 proceedings. The important matter is that this aspect of the case proceeds in such a way that the court has jurisdiction at a preliminary stage under s 14.

---

[33]   Procedure: CPR 1998 Part 8.

# 7. FUNDING FAMILY PROCEEDINGS

## INTRODUCTION

### Payment for legal advice and representation in family proceedings

**7.1**    If an ancillary relief application starts off on the footing that each party bears its own costs, it will be more important than ever before for the client and the solicitor to be clear as to how the application is to be funded. It is therefore assumed here that it is of the essence of a solicitor's retainer that he or she be paid for work which is undertaken for the client. How to fund legal advice and representation for ancillary relief proceedings is generally a problem – sometimes acute – for all clients, save perhaps the very wealthy, and, for very different reasons, those with a legal aid (public funding) certificate.

**7.2**    Broadly, there will be six ways of funding advice and representation for family proceedings:

(1)    payment in cash;
(2)    legal aid;
(3)    borrowing – whether from family, friends or a commercial institution;
(4)    payment by interim court order (financial provision as lump sum or periodical payments) from the other spouse;
(5)    funding of the case by legal representatives – whether by assignment of the benefit of any lump sum or by lien or charge on the ultimate proceeds of the case;
(6)    costs orders at the conclusion of the application – whether against the other party, the Legal Services Commission or other third party or as a result of a wasted costs order.

**7.3**    Of these means of payment:

- this chapter considers payment by interim court order and funding of the case by legal representatives;
- payments by cash and by borrowing from third parties including commercial lenders will be a matter for individual arrangement in each case.

Because a party has a legal aid certificate does not, of itself, prevent the court from making an order for costs against that party. Such an order will be made under ordinary principles for costs orders.[1] In ancillary relief such orders will

---

[1]    CPR 1998 Part 44 (especially r 44.3) and FPR 1991 r 2.71 (for ancillary relief). Costs procedures generally are summarised in *Family Court Practice* Procedural Guides 79A–79G.

be rare, save if based on conduct. If the court would not normally make an order – for example, because of the no order for costs principle under Family Proceedings Rules (FPR) 1991 r 2.71(4) – then it cannot normally make an order for costs where that may be passed on to an order against the Legal Services Commission.[2]

### Interim costs orders

**7.4**     By interim costs order is meant an order for costs at an interlocutory or interim order stage (as distinct from an order that one party makes financial provision which is intended to go towards the other's legal expenses). There is no reason why such an order should not be made. It is likely that it will be decided on the same bases as any ancillary relief costs order: that is, broadly, no order for costs unless conduct can be proved.[3]

## INTERIM COSTS PROVISION

### Pre-amble: towards *White v White* on expenses provision?

**7.5**     As will be seen, much of the case-law, such as it is, on the subject of a party's legal expenses – 'costs allowance' – is expressed in the language of maintenance and of a dependency of one party on the other. These cases speak of provision of a 'costs allowance' and that such provision may be made in 'exceptional circumstances'. Why should this be? It will be recalled that, in one of its best known passages, under the heading 'Equality', Lord Nicholls of Birkenhead[4] set out his understanding of the ancillary relief jurisdiction as follows:

> '[T]here is one principle of universal application which can be stated with confidence. In seeking to achieve a fair outcome, there is no place for discrimination between husband and wife and their respective roles. Typically, a husband and wife share the activities of earning money, running their home and caring for their children ... But whatever the division of labour chosen by the husband and wife, or forced upon them by circumstances, fairness requires that this should not prejudice or advantage either party ... If, in their different spheres, each contributed equally to the family, then in principle it matters not which of them earned the money and built up the assets. There should be no bias in favour of the money-earner and against the home-maker and the child-carer ...
>
> A practical consideration follows from this. Sometimes, having carried out the statutory exercise, the judge's conclusion involves a more or less equal division of the available assets. More often, this is not so ... As a general guide, equality should be departed from only if, and to the extent that, there is good reason for doing so. The need to consider and articulate

---

2     *Keller v Keller and Legal Aid Board* [1995] 1 FLR 259, CA.
3     See Chapter 3.
4     In *White v White* [2001] 1 AC 596, [2000] 2 FLR 981 at 989.

reasons for departing from equality would help the parties and the court to focus on the need to ensure the absence of discrimination.

This is not to introduce a presumption of equal division under another guise. Generally accepted standards of fairness in a field such as this change and develop, sometimes quite radically, over comparatively short periods of time. The discretionary powers, conferred by Parliament 30 years ago, enable the courts to recognise and respond to developments of this sort. These wide powers enable the courts to make financial provision orders in tune with current perceptions of fairness. Today there is greater awareness of the value of non-financial contributions to the welfare of the family ... There is increased recognition that, by being at home and having and looking after young children, a wife may lose for ever the opportunity to acquire and develop her own money-earning qualifications and skills.'

**7.6** With the greatest respect to Thorpe LJ in *Taiga*,[5] and to Mr Nicholas Mostyn QC (in his role as a Deputy High Court judge), it is difficult to see why the same sentiments relating to equality of treatment by the courts should not inform a judge's considerations when he or she hears an application by the non-earning, non-owning spouse for financial provision – whether it be as periodical payments or interim lump sum under Matrimonial Causes Act 1973, s 23(3). As Lord Nicholls observes, it may be either one or the other party who earns the bread as against looking after the children. It may be an accident of private arrangement, it may be deliberate – it matters not which – that all the liquid assets from which costs can be paid are in one or other name; or that borrowing ability rests with one party only as against the other. Should not there be equality of opportunity as to employment of legal advisers – equality of arms, even – as between parties,[6] in the same way as there is intended to be fairness in final distribution?

## Interim funding of costs from other party

**7.7** An order for interim financial provision – otherwise called a 'costs allowance' – is not a costs order, in any sense of the term.[7] It cannot therefore fall foul of the provisions of r 2.71(4)(a). The question under consideration here is the provision from funds held by one spouse – or by both but one will not unlock the fund to pay the other's costs – cash or security, to make possible the funding of the other party's litigation. Payment can take two forms:

- from income: maintenance pending suit or interim periodical payments; or

- from capital: interim lump sum for expenses reasonably incurred.

---

[5] *Moses-Taiga v Taiga* [2005] EWCA Civ 1013 at [25]; and see extract in *TL v ML* (below).

[6] And see **7.13** below and the comments of Scarman LJ in *Calderbank v Calderbank* (below) on the subject of approaching the judgment table with equality.

[7] *TL v ML and others (Ancillary Relief: Claims against Assets of Extended Family)* [2005] EWHC 2860 (Fam), [2006] 1 FLR 864, Nicholas Mostyn QC sitting as a Deputy High Court judge at [127].

## 'Costs allowance'

**7.8** The present law on 'costs allowance' (ie a payment of maintenance pending suit or interim periodical payments, probably from the other spouse's income), is fully set out by Nicholas Mostyn QC in *TL v ML*.[8] In particular at [123]–[128] he held as follows:

'123. The leading cases as to the principles to be applied on an application for maintenance pending suit are *F v F (Ancillary Relief: Substantial Assets)* [1995] 2 FLR 45, *G v G (Maintenance Pending Suit: Legal Costs)* [2002] 3 FCR 339, and *M v M (Maintenance Pending Suit)* [2002] 2 FLR 123.

124. From these cases I derive the following principles:

i) The sole criterion to be applied in determining the application is "reasonableness" (s 22 Matrimonial Causes Act 1973), which, to my mind, is synonymous with "fairness".

ii) A very important factor in determining fairness is the marital standard of living (*F v F*). This is not to say that the exercise is merely to replicate that standard (*M v M*).

iii) In every maintenance pending suit application there should be a specific maintenance pending suit budget which excludes capital or long term expenditure more aptly to be considered on a final hearing (*F v F*). That budget should be examined critically in every case to exclude forensic exaggeration (*F v F*).

iv) Where the affidavit or Form E disclosure by the payer is obviously deficient the court should not hesitate to make robust assumptions about his ability to pay. The court is not confined to the mere say-so of the payer as to the extent of his income or resources (*G v G, M v M*). In such a situation the court should err in favour of the payee.

v) Where the paying party has historically been supported through the bounty of an outsider, and where the payer is asserting that the bounty had been curtailed but where the position of the outsider is ambiguous or unclear, then the court is justified in assuming that the third party will continue to supply the bounty, at least until final trial (*M v M*).

125. It seems to me that District Judge Maple applied these principles to the letter. H's maintenance pending suit affidavit was an unsatisfactory document – it exhibited statements of only one of his three Alpha bank accounts and implied that since June 2003 he had held no others. His Form E arrived on the date of the hearing, so late that neither Mr Amos nor the court had the opportunity to scrutinise it. CL's position was more than ambiguous – there was no direct evidence as to his stance whatever.

---

8    Ibid at [123]–[132].

126.   So far as the award of the costs allowance is concerned, at the time of the hearing the District Judge had only the benefit of the decisions in *A v A (Maintenance Pending Suit: Provision for legal costs)*, and *G v G (Maintenance Pending Suit: Legal Costs)* [2002] 3 FCR 339. Since then the Court of Appeal decision in *Moses-Taiga v Taiga* [2005] EWCA Civ 1013 (5 July 05) has been made. In that case Thorpe LJ stated:

> "[25] In construing section 22 as embracing the applicant's need for cash to finance the continuing litigation, and at least implicitly approving that practice, Mr Aderemi has quite rightly said that my observations in McFarlane were, strictly speaking, obiter. I accept that that is the correct classification. Nonetheless, the passage is a pretty clear indication of where I stand on this issue. In short, it seems to me that the progressive construction that the judges have adopted in the Family Division is both pragmatic and sensible. I accept that at the date of the advent of the Matrimonial Proceedings and Property Act 1970 (1 January 1971) no judge of the Division would have so construed section 22, particularly because one of the provisions of the 1970 Act was to remove the wife's agency of necessity and with it her opportunity to seek security for the costs of future litigation. But times have moved on. In the 1970s a petitioner who had no assets and whose only prospect of affluence lay in the outcome of her application for ancillary relief could easily find specialist solicitors who would pursue her claim on legal aid. That world has long since gone. In those days a number of the leading specialist ancillary relief firms could, as a matter of public duty, take on an admittedly small number of legally-aided cases. Leading firms that would not take legally-aided clients invariably had an arrangement to pass such cases to highly competent firms that would do legal aid. All those support systems have disappeared. The modern reality is that the highly specialist solicitors and counsel necessary for the conduct of big money cases will no longer do publicly-funded work. So if the applicant has no assets, can give no security for borrowings, cannot guarantee an outcome that would enable her to enter into an arrangement such as that which was upheld in Sears *Tooth v Payne Hicks Beach*, then there is no source of funding of the litigation other than the approach to the court for a maintenance pending suit that will include a substantial element to fund the cost of the litigation. Obviously in all these cases the dominant safeguard against injustice is the discretion of the trial judge, and it will only be in cases that are demonstrated to be exceptional that the court will consider exercising the jurisdiction. But I am in no doubt that in such exceptional cases section 22 can in modern times be construed to extend that far."

127.   Any doubt as to the legitimacy of the jurisdiction to award a costs allowance has now been laid to rest. It is clear that a costs allowance is not a costs order. It is a maintenance order that enables a party to fund the costs of her case. So, if and when the proposed reforms to the costs rules ever come into force, the general principle in those draft rules of "no order as to costs" will not apply to inhibit a court from awarding a costs allowance if it is otherwise appropriate to do so.

128.   Thorpe LJ speaks of the power only being exercised in "exceptional cases". I would be surprised if he intended by that remark to impose the need to demonstrate anything beyond the requirements that he had previously mentioned, namely, that the applicant (1) had no assets, and (2) could not raise a litigation loan, and (3) could not persuade her solicitors to enter into a *Sears Tooth v Payne Hicks Beach* charge. The combination of those three factors would, to my mind, make the case exceptional.'

**7.9**    The law, as found by Holman J in *A v A (Maintenance Pending Suit: Provision for Legal Fees),*[9] has therefore now been confirmed by the Court of Appeal. Further, the circumstances in which payment may be made have been fully explained. The next stage is to establish:

(1) Is the full panoply of evidence demanded by Thorpe LJ and Mr Mostyn[10] truly required in applications of this nature? Is the 'costs allowance' and 'maintenance' terminology appropriate? It smacks of discrimination by another route and in a context which would surely be discouraged by Lord Nicholls in the climate encouraged by him after *White*. (Apart from the discrimination against the non-earning party, the expense of the exercise described in these judgments would hardly be proportionate in any but the highest asset case.)

(2) Is it open to the court to make interim capital provision for payment of costs pending a final hearing? Mr Mostyn QC seemed to think not: he suggested a consensual arrangement for a payment on account where it was agreed that an applicant would recover a lump sum. Plainly the court could not compel this (nor did Mr Mostyn QC suggest that it could); and no provision is possible where, say, only property or pension might be recovered. (Mr Mostyn QC does not appear to have been referred to Matrimonial Causes Act 1973, s 23(3).)[11]

## Interim lump sum for expenses

**7.10**    Matrimonial Causes Act 1973, s 23(3) provides as follows:

'(3) Without prejudice to the generality of subsection (1)(c) or (f) [provision for lump sums on final decree for spouse and children] above–

(a)    an order under this section that a party to a marriage shall pay a lump sum to the other party may be made for the purpose of enabling that other party to meet any liabilities or expenses reasonably incurred by him or her in maintaining himself or herself or any child of the family before making an application for an order under this section in his or her favour;

---

9    [2002] 1 FLR 377.
10   *TL v ML* (above) at [128]–[130].
11   I am indebted to District Judge Bird for drawing s 23(3) to my attention many years ago. DJ Bird was a member of the PARAG which framed the recommendations which lead to the new costs rules. It must surely have been in the Group's mind that s 23(3) might be used in the way now proposed.

(b)   an order under this section for the payment of a lump sum to or for the benefit of a child of the family may be made for the purpose of enabling any liabilities or expenses reasonably incurred by or for the benefit of that child before the making of an application for an order under this section in his favour to be met; ...'

**7.11**   The court has clear powers to make interim lump sums for 'liabilities and expenses reasonably incurred'.[12] Expenses of 'maintaining' a party includes the payment of legal fees.[13] Costs do not actually have to have been paid to say they have been incurred.[14] The reference to 'before making an application for an order' must mean before the hearing of the application: failing that the provision can make no sense.

## Discrimination and the no costs order principle

**7.12**   The no costs order principle was partly driven by the post-*White* culture of seeking a yard-stick of equality: broad equality and fairness of provision in *White*, equality of misery (expenditure) on the question of costs. To deny – or to make difficult to achieve – equal availability of cash to pay legal costs from the totality of family resources would return to pre-*White* discrimination. Short extracts from the speech of Lord Nicholls cited above will suffice to illustrate the point:

'But whatever the division of labour chosen by the husband and wife, or forced upon them by circumstances, fairness requires that this should not prejudice or advantage either party ...'

'These wide powers enable the courts to make financial provision orders in tune with current perceptions of fairness.'

**7.13**   Perhaps the last word on equality, in terms of the parties' coming 'to the judgement seat', can be given to Scarman LJ (as he then was) in a case which is relevant elsewhere in this bulletin:[15]

'... [S]peaking for myself, I rejoice that it should be made abundantly plain that husbands and wives come to the judgment seat in matters of money and property upon a basis of complete equality. That complete equality may, and often will, have to give way to the particular circumstances of their married life. It does not follow that, because they come to the judgment seat on the basis of complete equality, justice requires an equal division of the assets. The proportion of the division is dependent upon circumstances. The assets have to be divided or financial provision made according to the guidelines set out in s 25. Every case will be different and no case may be decided except upon its particular facts.'

---

12   As was done for children in eg *Askew-Page v Page* [2001] Fam Law 794, HHJ Merton QC in Bristol County Court.

13   *Moses-Taiga v Taiga* [2005] EWCA Civ 1013.

14   *R v Clerk to Liverpool Magistrates' Court ex p McCormick* [2001] WLR, CA.

15   *Calderbank v Calderbank* (1975) FLR Rep 120. The judgment of Scarman LJ was concerned with a wife who introduced all the capital into a 17-year marriage and her objection that it was not for her to provide for her former husband's needs.

It would be a beneficent irony indeed if the new rules, which exclude from ancillary relief proceedings, as they seek to do, the costs principles in *Calderbank*, only then were able to find another of the central tenets of that case, enunciated over 30 years ago, being used to reinforce a search for fairness between the parties in the obtaining of legal assistance and representation in preparation for trial.

**7.14**   The spirit lauded by Scarman LJ in *Calderbank* is surely one which can be urged as a basis for helping both parties to pursue their applications with equality of arms, that is to 'come before the judgment seat … upon a basis of complete equality'. *White* deals with fairness of disposal. *Calderbank* and Scarman LJ deal with the fairness with which the court treats both parties as they pursue their application and bring that application before the court.

# FUNDING OF THE CASE BY SOLICITORS

## Introduction

**7.15**   Borrowing to fund a case can take a variety of forms: borrowing from family, friends or from a bank or other commercial institution; what amounts to borrowing from the client's solicitor; or, in a legal aid case where money or property has been recovered or preserved, borrowing from the taxpayer. It is to the question of the solicitor funding the litigation – as distinct from attempting to enter into an unenforceable conditional fee agreement[16] – that this section is addressed.

**7.16**   A solicitor's funding of family litigation takes two distinct forms: the security route, where a charge or lien is taken or is implied by statute or equity; or the assignment route. Here there may be an issue as to whether the legal representative – solicitor or barrister – may conceivably be regarded as being involved in a personal costs orders because he or she is treated as maintaining, or funding, the litigation.

## Champerty

**7.17**   Champerty, or financially supporting the litigation in one way or another, was defined by Lord Denning MR in *Trendtex Trading Corporation v Credit Suisse*[17] as:

> 'Modern public policy condemns champerty in a lawyer whenever he seeks to recover – not only his proper costs – but also a proportion of the damages for himself: or when he conducts a case on the basis that he is to be paid if he wins but not if he loses.'

---

16   Courts and Legal Services Act 1990, s 58A(1) and (2).

17   [1980] QB 629, CA at 654 (cited with approval by Wilson J as his preferred 'reasonably modern definition of champerty with specific reference to lawyers' in the *Sears Tooth* case at 128B).

In modern terms the second limb of Lord Denning's assessment amounts to a conditional fee agreement, now statutorily approved[18] in all litigation save family proceedings and almost all criminal proceedings. In each of these forms of proceedings a conditional fee agreement is unenforceable.[19]

**7.18** The question remains open as to whether merely making litigation possible is champerty. In this respect there is no agreement to share in the spoils, or an agreement by the legal representative that he or she is to be paid only if the claim is successful. The litigation proceeds because the legal representative, or anyone else (eg trades union, Legal Services Commission, family friend etc) agrees to assist a claimant with costs. Is such a person providing 'maintenance' in this context? The subject was carefully considered by Wilson J in the *Sears Tooth* case, and in circumstances – it must be said – where every possible point seems to have been taken against Messrs Seers Tooth by both defendants: Payne, Hicks Beach (the wife's former solicitors) and the former husband, alike – or so the judgment suggests. He rejected the contention that solicitors in circumstances where they assist a client by delaying payment of their costs until conclusion of the proceedings can be held to have in any way a champertous relationship with their client or the client's litigation.

**The solicitors' lien**

**7.19** The common law lien and the equitable lien are two different legal creatures. The common law lien depends upon possession: it enables a person to retain possession of something belonging to another person until the second person has satisfied a claim. The equitable lien creates a charge upon property of the debtor until claims are satisfied. (The equitable lien is given statutory shape in the legal aid statutory charge.)[20] It therefore does not depend upon possession of goods for its existence and can be enforced by order of sale.

**7.20** The solicitor's lien for his or her costs can operate as both types of lien. First, the solicitor has a common law lien over property held by the solicitor: for example, money in a client's account, papers held for a client. It is a general lien, in that it covers all costs due from the client to the solicitor, not just the costs in the proceedings or other transaction to which the money or property is related. Alongside this the solicitor has an equitable lien over property recovered or preserved through the solicitor's efforts, generally (though not exclusively) in litigation. This lien did not extend to real property, but has been so extended by statute under the Solicitors Act 1974, s 73.

**Solicitors Act 1974, s 73**

**7.21** The Solicitors Act 1974, s 73 creates a statutory lien upon 'property [whether realty or personalty] recovered or preserved through [the solicitor's] instrumentality for his taxed costs' in any proceedings prosecuted or defended

---

18  Courts and Legal Services Act 1990, s 58.
19  A solicitor may not enter into 'an enforceable conditional fee agreement' in respect of 'family proceedings' (Courts and Legal Services Act 1990, s 58A(1) and (2)).
20  Access to Justice Act 1999, s 10(8).

by the solicitor for his or her client. However, the 'solicitor [becomes] entitled to a charge' by operation of a court order in respect of taxed costs. Thus, whilst the equitable common law lien operates for all costs by law and the equitable lien operates on property (other than realty) for those costs, the statutory lien involves the solicitor in a two-stage court process: detailed assessment of his or her bill and application for the charge. (There seems no reason why both processes – detailed assessment of costs and application for a charge – should not be run together; nor why the application for a charge under s 73 should not be made, for example, at the end of the hearing in which the property is recovered or preserved.)[21]

## The assignment route

**7.22**    An assignment, properly so called, operates to assign the benefit of a chose in action. The essence of the chose in action is present existence, a condition precedent of such existence being one or more remedies for its enforcement. What amounts to a hope of future benefit or expectancy is not a chose in action and cannot be assigned at law or in equity; whereas a present contingent right or expectation (a right to claim damages, which may or may not succeed, an expectation of inheritance) are not capable of assignment.

**7.23**    *Sears Tooth v Payne Hicks Beach and others*[22] was concerned with a wife whose income made her ineligible for legal aid, but who had no means to pursue her ancillary relief claim.

> 'How is complex litigation to be funded for claimants who, although ineligible for legal aid, are unable to fund it out of their own resources and whose opponents are economically stronger and well able to take tactical advantage of the imbalance? … If lawyers [for such claimants] are prepared to take such cases on credit, without either substantial payments on account or security, their clients are indeed fortunate … While payment must be made in any event, it will in the first instance be made *out of the capital awarded to the wife* [the judge's italics] … Arrangements which induce solicitors to extend the indulgence of credit to impecunious wives are in principle very much in the public interest.'[23]

**7.24**    Wilson J concluded that the wife in this instance had assigned 'a future chose in action' namely 'the fruits of her claim' for a lump sum.[24] If she had assigned the right to claim, that would have been against public policy. Any assignment on that basis would be unenforceable; but such an assignment can be distinguished from the *Sears Tooth*, where there is an assignment of the fruit of that claim. In the assignment of the right to claim, the assignee acquires the right to sue for someone else (which amounts to a form of champerty); whereas in the latter it is open to the assignor to abandon the litigation or pursue it, as

---

21   A precedent for such an order might be as follows: 'For the purposes only of the [petitioner's/respondent's] retainer with his/her solicitors [*name of solicitors*] and pursuant to Solicitor's Act 1974, s 73 the solicitors do have a charge over the interest of the [petitioner/respondent] in the lump sum/property recovered or preserved by the [petitioner/respondent] under paragraph[s] [...] of this order.'

22   [1997] 2 FLR 116 Wilson J.

23   Per Wilson J at 128D, 128F–G and 129E.

24   *Sears Tooth v Payne Hicks Beach and others* (above) per Wilson J at 124G–125G following the Court of Appeal decision in *Glegg v Bromley* [1912] 3 KB 474.

she sees fit; and the assignment is contingent entirely upon her seeing through her claim.[25]

## Solicitors' lien by consent

**7.25** In *Sears Tooth* Wilson J makes brief reference to the Solicitors Act 1974, s 73 and says he doubts – though he accepts that the point was not argued before him – whether application under s 73 can be made 'in advance of the award'.[26] If s 73 is indeed a statutory expression of the lien then this must be right. A compromise might be to accept instructions from a client on terms – with separate advice if need be – that they sign, in advance of litigation, an agreement to a s 73 charge. This agreement, expressed as a court order, would then be placed before the court in the event of property being recovered or preserved, and whether as part of a consent order or at the conclusion of contested proceedings. It is an assignment of the fruits of the proceedings[27] and therefore its existence, says Wilson J, should be drawn to the attention of the court and the other spouse (and any other parties).

25 *Glegg v Bromley* (above) explained by Wilson J in *Sears Tooth v Payne Hicks Beach and others* at 124B–F.
26 At 130A–B.
27 *Sears Tooth* (above) at 133H–134A.

# APPENDIX

Supreme Court Act 1981, s 51      81

Civil Procedure Rules 1998, Part 1, rr 2.1, 2.3, 2.8, 3.9, Part 44 (except rr 44.6, 44.8–44.12, 44.15–44.16) and r 48.7      83

Family Proceedings Rules 1991, rr 2.51B, 2.61E, 2.61F, 2.69E, 2.71      95

Family Proceedings (Amendment) Rules 2006      99

Practice Directions
  CPR Costs PD – Sections 8, 11, 18, 53      109
  Family PDs
    *President's Direction of 25 May 2000* [2000] 1 FLR 997      115
    *President's Direction of 24 July 2000* [2000] 2 FLR 428      121
    *President's Direction of 20 February 2006* [2006] 1 FLR 864      123

# SUPREME COURT ACT 1981

****

## *Costs*

### 51 Costs in civil division of Court of Appeal, High Court and county courts

(1) Subject to the provisions of this or any other enactment and to rules of court, the costs of and incidental to all proceedings in –

(a)    the civil division of the Court of Appeal;

(b)    the High Court; and

(c)    any county court,

shall be in the discretion of the court.

(2) Without prejudice to any general power to make rules of court, such rules may make provision for regulating matters relating to the costs of those proceedings including, in particular, prescribing scales of costs to be paid to legal or other representatives or for securing that the amount awarded to a party in respect of the costs to be paid by him to such representatives is not limited to what would have been payable by him to them if he had not been awarded costs.

(3) The court shall have full power to determine by whom and to what extent the costs are to be paid.

(4) In subsections (1) and (2) 'proceedings' includes the administration of estates and trusts.

(5) Nothing in subsection (1) shall alter the practice in any criminal cause, or in bankruptcy.

(6) In any proceedings mentioned in subsection (1), the court may disallow, or (as the case may be) order the legal or other representative concerned to meet, the whole of any wasted costs or such part of them as may be determined in accordance with rules of court.

(7) In subsection (6), 'wasted costs' means any costs incurred by a party –

(a)    as a result of any improper, unreasonable or negligent act or omission on the part of any legal or other representative or any employee of such a representative; or

(b)    which, in the light of any such act or omission occurring after they were incurred, the court considers it is unreasonable to expect that party to pay.

(8) Where –

(a)    a person has commenced proceedings in the High Court; but

(b)    those proceedings should, in the opinion of the court, have been commenced in a county court in accordance with any provision made under section 1 of the Courts and Legal Services Act 1990 or by or under any other enactment,

the person responsible for determining the amount which is to be awarded to that person by way of costs shall have regard to those circumstances.

(9)  Where, in complying with subsection (8), the responsible person reduces the amount which would otherwise be awarded to the person in question –

> (*a*)      the amount of that reduction shall not exceed 25 per cent; and

> (*b*)      on any taxation of the costs payable by that person to his legal representative, regard shall be had to the amount of the reduction.

(10) The Lord Chancellor may by order amend subsection (9)(*a*) by substituting, for the percentage for the time being mentioned there, a different percentage.

(11)  Any such order shall be made by statutory instrument and may make such transitional or incidental provision as the Lord Chancellor considers expedient.

(12)  No such statutory instrument shall be made unless a draft of the instrument has been approved by both Houses of Parliament.

(13)  In this section 'legal or other representative', in relation to a party to proceedings, means any person exercising a right of audience or right to conduct litigation on his behalf.

**Amendments**—Courts and Legal Services Act 1990, s 4(1); Access to Justice Act 1999, s 31.

****

# CIVIL PROCEDURE RULES 1998

## SI 1998/3132

### PART 1
### OVERRIDING OBJECTIVE

### 1.1 The overriding objective

(1) These Rules are a new procedural code with the overriding objective of enabling the court to deal with cases justly.

(2) Dealing with a case justly includes, so far as is practicable –

    (*a*)    ensuring that the parties are on an equal footing;

    (*b*)    saving expense;

    (*c*)    dealing with the case in ways which are proportionate –

        (i)    to the amount of money involved;

        (ii)    to the importance of the case;

        (iii)    to the complexity of the issues; and

        (iv)    to the financial position of each party;

    (*d*)    ensuring that it is dealt with expeditiously and fairly; and

    (*e*)    allotting to it an appropriate share of the court's resources, while taking into account the need to allot resources to other cases.

### 1.2 Application by the court of the overriding objective

The court must seek to give effect to the overriding objective when it –

    (*a*)    exercises any power given to it by the Rules; or

    (*b*)    interprets any rule, subject to rule 76.2.

Amendment—SI 2005/656.

### 1.3 Duty of the parties

The parties are required to help the court to further the overriding objective.

### 1.4 Court's duty to manage cases

(1) The court must further the overriding objective by actively managing cases.

(2) Active case management includes –

    (*a*)    encouraging the parties to co-operate with each other in the conduct of the proceedings;

    (*b*)    identifying the issues at an early stage;

(*c*)      deciding promptly which issues need full investigation and trial and accordingly disposing summarily of the others;

(*d*)      deciding the order in which issues are to be resolved;

(*e*)      encouraging the parties to use an alternative dispute resolution(GL) procedure if the court considers that appropriate and facilitating the use of such procedure;

(*f*)      helping the parties to settle the whole or part of the case;

(*g*)      fixing timetables or otherwise controlling the progress of the case;

(*h*)      considering whether the likely benefits of taking a particular step justify the cost of taking it;

(*i*)      dealing with as many aspects of the case as it can on the same occasion;

(*j*)      dealing with the case without the parties needing to attend at court;

(*k*)      making use of technology; and

(*l*)      giving directions to ensure that the trial of a case proceeds quickly and efficiently.

## PART 2
## APPLICATION AND INTERPRETATION OF THE RULES

### 2.1 Application of the Rules

(1) Subject to paragraph (2), these Rules apply to all proceedings in –

(*a*)      county courts;

(*b*)      the High Court; and

(*c*)      the Civil Division of the Court of Appeal.

(2) These Rules do not apply to proceedings of the kinds specified in the first column of the following Table (proceedings for which rules may be made under the enactments specified in the second column) except to the extent that they are applied to those proceedings by another enactment –

| Proceedings | Enactments |
|---|---|
| 1. Insolvency proceedings | Insolvency Act 1986, ss 411 and 412 |
| 2. Non-contentious or common form probate proceedings | Supreme Court Act 1981, s 127 |
| 3. Proceedings in the High Court when acting as a Prize Court | Prize Courts Act 1894, s 3 |
| 4. Proceedings before the judge within the meaning of Part VII of the Mental Health Act 1983 | Mental Health Act 1983, s 106 |
| 5. Family proceedings | Matrimonial and Family Proceedings Act 1984, s 40 |
| 6. Adoption proceedings | Adoption Act 1976, s 66 or Adoption and Children Act 2002, s 141 |
| 7. Election petitions in the High Court | Representation of the People Act 1983, s 182 |

**Amendments**—SI 1999/1008; SI 2003/1242; SI 2005/3515.

## 2.3 Interpretation

(1) In these Rules –

'child' has the meaning given by rule 21.1(2);

'civil restraint order' means an order restraining a party –

    (*a*)    from making any further applications in current proceedings (a limited civil restraint order);

    (*b*)    from issuing certain claims or making certain applications in specified courts (an extended civil restraint order); or

    (*c*)    from issuing any claim or making any application in specified courts (a general civil restraint order).

'claim for personal injuries' means proceedings in which there is a claim for damages in respect of personal injuries to the claimant or any other person or in respect of a person's death, and 'personal injuries' includes any disease and any impairment of a person's physical or mental condition;

'claimant' means a person who makes a claim;

'CCR' is to be interpreted in accordance with Part 50;

'court officer' means a member of the court staff;

'defendant' means a person against whom a claim is made;

'defendant's home court' means –

    (*a*)    if the claim is proceeding in a county court, the county court for the district in which the defendant resides or carries on business; and

    (*b*)    if the claim is proceeding in the High Court, the district registry for the district in which the defendant resides or carries on business or, where there is no such district registry, the Royal Courts of Justice;

(Rule 6.5 provides for a party to give an address for service)

'filing', in relation to a document, means delivering it, by post or otherwise, to the court office;

'judge' means, unless the context otherwise requires, a judge, Master or district judge or a person authorised to act as such;

'jurisdiction' means, unless the context requires otherwise, England and Wales and any part of the territorial waters of the United Kingdom adjoining England and Wales;

'legal representative' means a barrister or a solicitor, solicitor's employee or other authorised litigator (as defined in the Courts and Legal Services Act 1990) who has been instructed to act for a party in relation to a claim.

'litigation friend' has the meaning given by Part 21;

'patient' has the meaning given by rule 21.1(2);

'RSC' is to be interpreted in accordance with Part 50;

'statement of case' –

    (*a*)    means a claim form, particulars of claim where these are not included in a claim form, defence, Part 20 claim, or reply to defence; and

    (*b*)    includes any further information given in relation to them voluntarily or by court order under rule 18.1;

'statement of value' is to be interpreted in accordance with rule 16.3;

'summary judgment' is to be interpreted in accordance with Part 24.

(2) A reference to a 'specialist list' is a reference to a list(GL) that has been designated as such by a rule or practice direction.

(3) Where the context requires, a reference to 'the court' means a reference to a particular county court, a district registry, or the Royal Courts of Justice.

**Amendments**—SI 2000/2092; SI 2001/4015; SI 2004/2072.

****

## 2.8 Time

(1) This rule shows how to calculate any period of time for doing any act which is specified –

(a)    by these Rules;

(b)    by a practice direction; or

(c)    by a judgment or order of the court.

(2)  A period of time expressed as a number of days shall be computed as clear days.

(3)  In this rule 'clear days' means that in computing the number of days –

(a)    the day on which the period begins; and

(b)    if the end of the period is defined by reference to an event, the day on which that event occurs

are not included.

Examples

(i)    Notice of an application must be served at least 3 days before the hearing.

An application is to be heard on Friday 20 October.

The last date for service is Monday 16 October.

(ii)    The court is to fix a date for a hearing.

The hearing must be at least 28 days after the date of notice.

If the court gives notice of the date of the hearing on 1 October, the earliest date for the hearing is 30 October.

(iii)    Particulars of claim must be served within 14 days of service of the claim form.

The claim form is served on 2 October.

The last day for service of the particulars of claim is 16 October.

(4)  Where the specified period –

(a)    is 5 days or less; and

(b)    includes –

(i)    a Saturday or Sunday; or

(ii)    a Bank Holiday, Christmas Day or Good Friday,

that day does not count.

Example

Notice of an application must be served at least 3 days before the hearing.

An application is to be heard on Monday 20 October.

The last date for service is Tuesday 14 October.

(5)  When the period specified –

(a)    by these Rules or a practice direction; or

(b)    by any judgment or court order,

for doing any act at the court office ends on a day on which the office is closed, that act shall be in time if done on the next day on which the court office is open.

\*\*\*\*

## PART 3
### THE COURT'S CASE MANAGEMENT POWERS

\*\*\*\*

### 3.9 Relief from sanctions

(1) On an application for relief from any sanction imposed for a failure to comply with any rule, practice direction or court order the court will consider all the circumstances including –

    (*a*)        the interests of the administration of justice;

    (*b*)        whether the application for relief has been made promptly;

    (*c*)        whether the failure to comply was intentional;

    (*d*)        whether there is a good explanation for the failure;

    (*e*)        the extent to which the party in default has complied with other rules, practice directions, court orders and any relevant pre-action protocol[(GL)];

    (*f*)        whether the failure to comply was caused by the party or his legal representative;

    (*g*)        whether the trial date or the likely trial date can still be met if relief is granted;

    (*h*)        the effect which the failure to comply had on each party; and

    (*i*)        the effect which the granting of relief would have on each party.

(2) An application for relief must be supported by evidence.

\*\*\*\*

## PART 44
### GENERAL RULES ABOUT COSTS

### 44.1 Scope of this Part

This Part contains general rules about costs and entitlement to costs.

    (The definitions contained in Part 43 are relevant to this Part)

### 44.2 Solicitor's duty to notify client

Where –

    (*a*)        the court makes a costs order against a legally represented party; and

    (*b*)        the party is not present when the order is made,

the party's solicitor must notify his client in writing of the costs order no later than 7 days after the solicitor receives notice of the order.

**44.3  Court's discretion and circumstances to be taken into account when exercising its discretion as to costs**

(1)  The court has discretion as to –

  (*a*)      whether costs are payable by one party to another;

  (*b*)      the amount of those costs; and

  (*c*)      when they are to be paid.

(2)  If the court decides to make an order about costs –

  (*a*)      the general rule is that the unsuccessful party will be ordered to pay the costs of the successful party; but

  (*b*)      the court may make a different order.

(3)  The general rule does not apply to the following proceedings –

  (*a*)      proceedings in the Court of Appeal on an application or appeal made in connection with proceedings in the Family Division; or

  (*b*)      proceedings in the Court of Appeal from a judgment, direction, decision or order given or made in probate proceedings or family proceedings.

(4)  In deciding what order (if any) to make about costs, the court must have regard to all the circumstances, including –

  (*a*)      the conduct of all the parties;

  (*b*)      whether a party has succeeded on part of his case, even if he has not been wholly successful; and

  (*c*)      any payment into court or admissible offer to settle made by a party which is drawn to the court's attention (whether or not made in accordance with Part 36).

  (Part 36 contains further provisions about how the court's discretion is to be exercised where a payment into court or an offer to settle is made under that Part)

(5)  The conduct of the parties includes –

  (*a*)      conduct before, as well as during, the proceedings and in particular the extent to which the parties followed any relevant pre-action protocol;

  (*b*)      whether it was reasonable for a party to raise, pursue or contest a particular allegation or issue;

  (*c*)      the manner in which a party has pursued or defended his case or a particular allegation or issue; and

  (*d*)      whether a claimant who has succeeded in his claim, in whole or in part, exaggerated his claim.

(6)  The orders which the court may make under this rule include an order that a party must pay –

  (*a*)      a proportion of another party's costs;

  (*b*)      a stated amount in respect of another party's costs;

  (*c*)      costs from or until a certain date only;

  (*d*)      costs incurred before proceedings have begun;

>   (*e*)     costs relating to particular steps taken in the proceedings;
>
>   (*f*)     costs relating only to a distinct part of the proceedings; and
>
>   (*g*)     interest on costs from or until a certain date, including a date before judgment.

(7) Where the court would otherwise consider making an order under paragraph (6)(*f*), it must instead, if practicable, make an order under paragraph (6)(*a*) or (*c*).

(8) Where the court has ordered a party to pay costs, it may order an amount to be paid on account before the costs are assessed.

(9) Where a party entitled to costs is also liable to pay costs the court may assess the costs which that party is liable to pay and either –

>   (*a*)     set off the amount assessed against the amount the party is entitled to be paid and direct him to pay any balance; or
>
>   (*b*)     delay the issue of a certificate for the costs to which the party is entitled until he has paid the amount which he is liable to pay.

****

## 44.4  Basis of assessment

(1) Where the court is to assess the amount of costs (whether by summary or detailed assessment) it will assess those costs –

>   (*a*)     on the standard basis; or
>
>   (*b*)     on the indemnity basis,

but the court will not in either case allow costs which have been unreasonably incurred or are unreasonable in amount.

>   (Rule 48.3 sets out how the court decides the amount of costs payable under a contract)

(2) Where the amount of costs is to be assessed on the standard basis, the court will –

>   (*a*)     only allow costs which are proportionate to the matters in issue; and
>
>   (*b*)     resolve any doubt which it may have as to whether costs were reasonably incurred or reasonable and proportionate in amount in favour of the paying party.

>   (Factors which the court may take into account are set out in rule 44.5)

(3) Where the amount of costs is to be assessed on the indemnity basis, the court will resolve any doubt which it may have as to whether costs were reasonably incurred or were reasonable in amount in favour of the receiving party.

(4) Where –

>   (*a*)     the court makes an order about costs without indicating the basis on which the costs are to be assessed; or
>
>   (*b*)     the court makes an order for costs to be assessed on a basis other than the standard basis or the indemnity basis,

the costs will be assessed on the standard basis.

(5) (*revoked*)

(6) …

**Amendments**—SI 2000/1317.

### 44.5　Factors to be taken into account in deciding the amount of costs

(1)　The court is to have regard to all the circumstances in deciding whether costs were –

        (*a*)　　if it is assessing costs on the standard basis –

                (i)　　proportionately and reasonably incurred; or

                (ii)　　were proportionate and reasonable in amount, or

        (*b*)　　if it is assessing costs on the indemnity basis –

                (i)　　unreasonably incurred; or

                (ii)　　unreasonable in amount.

(2)　In particular the court must give effect to any orders which have already been made.

(3)　The court must also have regard to –

        (*a*)　　the conduct of all the parties, including in particular –

                (i)　　conduct before, as well as during, the proceedings; and

                (ii)　　the efforts made, if any, before and during the proceedings in order to try to resolve the dispute;

        (*b*)　　the amount or value of any money or property involved;

        (*c*)　　the importance of the matter to all the parties;

        (*d*)　　the particular complexity of the matter or the difficulty or novelty of the questions raised;

        (*e*)　　the skill, effort, specialised knowledge and responsibility involved;

        (*f*)　　the time spent on the case; and

        (*g*)　　the place where and the circumstances in which work or any part of it was done.

    (Rule 35.4(4) gives the court power to limit the amount that a party may recover with regard to the fees and expenses of an expert)

\*\*\*\*

### 44.7　Procedure for assessing costs

Where the court orders a party to pay costs to another party (other than fixed costs) it may either –

        (*a*)　　make a summary assessment of the costs; or

        (*b*)　　order detailed assessment of the costs by a costs officer,

unless any rule, practice direction or other enactment provides otherwise.

    (The costs practice direction sets out the factors which will affect the court's decision under this rule)

\*\*\*\*

## 44.13 Special situations

(1) Where the court makes an order which does not mention costs –

    (*a*)    subject to paragraphs (1A) and (1B), the general rule is that no party is entitled to costs in relation to that order; but

    (*b*)    this does not affect any entitlement of a party to recover costs out of a fund held by him as trustee or personal representative, or pursuant to any lease, mortgage or other security.

(1A) Where the court makes –

    (*a*)    an order granting permission to appeal;

    (*b*)    an order granting permission to apply for judicial review; or

    (*c*)    any other order or direction sought by a party on an application without notice, and its order does not mention costs, it will be deemed to include an order for applicant's costs in the case.

(1B) Any party affected by a deemed order for costs under paragraph (1A) may apply at any time to vary the order.

(2) The court hearing an appeal may, unless it dismisses the appeal, make orders about the costs of the proceedings giving rise to the appeal as well as the costs of the appeal.

(3) Where proceedings are transferred from one court to another, the court to which they are transferred may deal with all the costs, including the costs before the transfer.

(4) Paragraph (3) is subject to any order of the court which ordered the transfer.

**Amendments**—SI 2001/4015; SI 2005/2292.

## 44.14 Court's powers in relation to misconduct

(1) The court may make an order under this rule where –

    (*a*)    a party or his legal representative, in connection with a summary or detailed assessment, fails to comply with a rule, practice direction or court order; or

    (*b*)    it appears to the court that the conduct of a party or his legal representative, before or during the proceedings which gave rise to the assessment proceedings, was unreasonable or improper.

(2) Where paragraph (1) applies, the court may –

    (*a*)    disallow all or part of the costs which are being assessed; or

    (*b*)    order the party at fault or his legal representative to pay costs which he has caused any other party to incur.

(3) Where –

    (*a*)    the court makes an order under paragraph (2) against a legally represented party; and

    (*b*)    the party is not present when the order is made,

the party's solicitor must notify his client in writing of the order no later than 7 days after the solicitor receives notice of the order.

    (Other rules about costs can be found –

(a)     in Schedule 1, in the following RSC Ord 45 (court may order act to be done at the expense of disobedient party); Ord 47 (writ of fieri facias to enforce payment of costs); and

(b)     in Schedule 2, in the following CCR Ord 27 (attachment of earnings – judgment creditor's entitlement to costs); Ord 28 (costs on judgment summons); Ord 30 (garnishee proceedings – judgment creditor's entitlement to costs); Ord 49 (costs incurred in making a payment in under section 63 of the Trustee Act 1925 to be assessed by the detailed procedure))

**Amendments**—SI 2000/1317.

****

### 44.17  Application of costs rules

This Part and Part 45 (fixed costs), Part 46 (fast track trial costs, Part 47 (procedure for detailed assessment of costs and default provisions) and Part 48 (special cases), do not apply to the assessment of costs in proceedings to the extent that –

(a)     section 11 of the Access to Justice Act 1999, and the provisions made under that Act; or

(b)     regulations made under the Legal Aid Act 1988;

make different provision.

(The costs practice direction sets out the procedure to be followed where a party was wholly or partially funded by the Legal Services Commission.)

**Amendments**—Inserted by SI 2000/1317.

****

## PART 48
### COSTS – SPECIAL CASES

(The definitions contained in Part 43 are relevant to this Part)

****

### 48.7  Personal liability of legal representative for costs – wasted costs orders

(1) This rule applies where the court is considering whether to make an order under section 51(6) of the Supreme Court Act 1981 (court's power to disallow or (as the case may be) order a legal representative to meet, 'wasted costs').

(2) The court must give the legal representative a reasonable opportunity to attend a hearing to give reasons why it should not make such an order.

(3) (*revoked*)

(4) When the court makes a wasted costs order, it must –

(a)     specify the amount to be disallowed or paid; or

(b)      direct a costs judge or a district judge to decide the amount of costs to be disallowed or paid.

(5) The court may direct that notice must be given to the legal representative's client, in such manner as the court may direct –

(a)      of any proceedings under this rule; or

(b)      of any order made under it against his legal representative.

(6) Before making a wasted costs order, the court may direct a costs judge or a district judge to inquire into the matter and report to the court.

(7) The court may refer the question of wasted costs to a costs judge or a district judge, instead of making a wasted costs order.

**Amendments**—SI 2000/1317; SI 2002/2058.

\*\*\*\*

# FAMILY PROCEEDINGS RULES 1991

## SI 1991/1247

\*\*\*\*

### 2.51B  Application of ancillary relief rules

(1)  The procedures set out in rules 2.51D to 2.71 ('the ancillary relief rules') apply to –

    (*a*)        any ancillary relief application,

    (*b*)        any application under section 10(2) of the Act of 1973, and

    (*c*)        any application under section 48(2) of the Act of 2004.

(2)  In the ancillary relief rules, unless the context otherwise requires:

'applicant' means the party applying for ancillary relief;
'respondent' means the respondent to the application for ancillary relief;
'FDR appointment' means a Financial Dispute Resolution appointment in accordance with rule 2.61E.

**Amendments**—Inserted by SI 1999/3491; amended by SI 2005/2922; SI 2006/352.

\*\*\*\*

### 2.61E  The FDR appointment

(1)  The FDR appointment must be treated as a meeting held for the purposes of discussion and negotiation and paragraphs (2) to (9) apply.

(2)  The district judge or judge hearing the FDR appointment must have no further involvement with the application, other than to conduct any further FDR appointment or to make a consent order or a further directions order.

(3)  Not later than 7 days before the FDR appointment, the applicant must file with the court details of all offers and proposals, and responses to them.

(4)  Paragraph (3) includes any offers, proposals or responses made wholly or partly without prejudice, but paragraph (3) does not make any material admissible as evidence if, but for that paragraph, it would not be admissible.

(5)  At the conclusion of the FDR appointment, any documents filed under paragraph (3), and any filed documents referring to them, must, at the request of the party who filed them, be returned to him and not retained on the court file.

(6)  Parties attending the FDR appointment must use their best endeavours to reach agreement on the matters in issue between them.

(7)  The FDR appointment may be adjourned from time to time.

(8)  At the conclusion of the FDR appointment, the court may make an appropriate consent order, but otherwise must give directions for the future course of the proceedings, including, where appropriate, the filing of evidence and fixing a final hearing date.

(9) Both parties must personally attend the FDR appointment unless the court orders otherwise.

**Amendments**—Inserted by SI 1999/3491.

### 2.61F  Costs

(1) Subject to paragraph (2), at every hearing or appointment each party must produce to the court an estimate in Form H of the costs incurred by him up to the date of that hearing or appointment.

(2) Not less than 14 days before the date fixed for the final hearing of an application for ancillary relief, each party must (unless the court directs otherwise) file with the court and serve on each other party a statement in Form H1 giving full particulars of all costs in respect of the proceedings which he has incurred or expects to incur, to enable the court to take account of the parties' liabilities for costs when deciding what order (if any) to make for ancillary relief.

**Amendments**—Inserted by SI 1999/3491; SI 2006/352.

****

### 2.69E  Open proposals

(1) Not less than 14 days before the date fixed for the final hearing of an application for ancillary relief, the applicant must (unless the court directs otherwise) file with the court and serve on the respondent an open statement which sets out concise details, including the amounts involved, of the orders which he proposes to ask the court to make.

(2)  Not more than 7 days after service of a statement under paragraph (1), the respondent must file with the court and serve on the applicant an open statement which sets out concise details, including the amounts involved, of the orders which he proposes to ask the court to make.

**Amendments**—Inserted by SI 1999/3491.

****

### 2.71 Costs orders

(1) CPR rule 44.3(1) to (5) shall not apply to ancillary relief proceedings.

(2) CPR rule 44.3(6) to (9) apply to an order made under this rule as they apply to an order made under CPR rule 44.3.

(3) In this rule 'costs' has the same meaning as in CPR rule 43.2(1)(*a*) and includes the costs payable by a client to his solicitor.

(4)

> (*a*)      The general rule in ancillary relief proceedings is that the court will not make an order requiring one party to pay the costs of another party; but

> (*b*)      the court may make such an order at any stage of the proceedings where it considers it appropriate to do so because of the conduct of a party in relation to the proceedings (whether before or during them).

(5) In deciding what order (if any) to make under paragraph (4)(*b*), the court must have regard to—

(a)     any failure by a party to comply with these Rules, any order of the court or any practice direction which the court considers relevant;

(b)     any open offer to settle made by a party;

(c)     whether it was reasonable for a party to raise, pursue or contest a particular allegation or issue;

(d)     the manner in which a party has pursued or responded to the application or a particular allegation or issue;

(e)     any other aspect of a party's conduct in relation to the proceedings which the court considers relevant; and

(f)     the financial effect on the parties of any costs order.

(6) No offer to settle which is not an open offer to settle shall be admissible at any stage of the proceedings, except as provided by rule 2.61E.

**Amendments**—Inserted by SI 2006/352.

\*\*\*\*

# FAMILY PROCEEDINGS (AMENDMENT) RULES 2006

## SI 2006/352

### 1 Citation, commencement and interpretation

(1) These Rules may be cited as the Family Proceedings (Amendment) Rules 2006 and shall come into force on 3rd April 2006.

(2) In these Rules a reference to a rule or Appendix by number alone is a reference to the rule or Appendix so numbered in the Family Proceedings Rules 1991([1]) ('the 1991 Rules') and a form referred to by letters means the form so designated in Appendix 1A to those Rules.

### 2 Amendments to the 1991 Rules

In the arrangement of rules—

(a)     omit the entries relating to—

(i)     rule 2.69;

(ii)     rule 2.69B; and

(iii)     rule 2.69D; and

(b)     after the entry relating to rule 2.70 insert—

"2.71 Costs orders".

3 In rule 2.45(5) and (5A) and rule 2.51B(1), for '2.70', on each occasion it appears, substitute '2.71'.

4 In rule 2.61D(2), for sub-paragraph (e) substitute—

'(e)     in considering whether to make a costs order under rule 2.71(4), must have particular regard to the extent to which each party has complied with the requirement to send documents with Form E; and".

5 For rule 2.61F substitute—

'(1)     Subject to paragraph (2), at every hearing or appointment each party must produce to the court an estimate in Form H of the costs incurred by him up to the date of that hearing or appointment.

(2)     Not less than 14 days before the date fixed for the final hearing of an application for ancillary relief, each party must (unless the court directs otherwise) file with the court and serve on each other party a statement in Form H1 giving full particulars of all costs in respect of the proceedings which he has incurred or expects to incur, to enable the court to take account of the parties' liabilities for costs when deciding what order (if any) to make for ancillary relief.".

6 Omit rules 2.69, 2.69B and 2.69D.

---

[1]     S.1. 1991/1247; relevant amending instruments are S.I. 1991/2113, 1992/456, 1992/2067, 1993/295, 1994/3155, 1996/816, 1997/1056, 1998/1901, 2000/2267, 2001/821, 2003/184, 2003/2839, 2004/3375, 2005/264, 2005/412, 2005/559, 2005/1976, and 2005/2922.

7 After rule 2.70, insert—

**'Costs orders**

**2.71.**—(1) CPR rule 44.3(1) to (5) shall not apply to ancillary relief proceedings.

(2) CPR rule 44.3(6) to (9) apply to an order made under this rule as they apply to an order made under CPR rule 44.3.

(3) In this rule "costs" has the same meaning as in CPR rule 43.2(1)(a) and includes the costs payable by a client to his solicitor.

(4) (a) The general rule in ancillary relief proceedings is that the court will not make an order requiring one party to pay the costs of another party; but

    (b)  the court may make such an order at any stage of the proceedings where it considers it appropriate to do so because of the conduct of a party in relation to the proceedings (whether before or during them).

(5) In deciding what order (if any) to make under paragraph (4)(b), the court must have regard to—

    (a)  any failure by a party to comply with these Rules, any order of the court or any practice direction which the court considers relevant;

    (b)  any open offer to settle made by a party;

    (c)  whether it was reasonable for a party to raise, pursue or contest a particular allegation or issue;

    (d)  the manner in which a party has pursued or responded to the application or a particular allegation or issue;

    (e)  any other aspect of a party's conduct in relation to the proceedings which the court considers relevant; and

    (f)  the financial effect on the parties of any costs order.

(6) No offer to settle which is not an open offer to settle shall be admissible at any stage of the proceedings, except as provided by rule 2.61E.'.

8 In rule 10.27(1)—

    (a)     in sub-paragraph (b), for '.' substitute '; and'; and

    (b)     after sub-paragraph (b) insert—

    "(c) CPR rule 44.3(1) and (3) to (5) shall not apply to an application to which rule 2.71 (ancillary relief: costs) applies.".

9 In Appendix 1A—

    (a)     for Form H substitute Form H (Estimate of Costs (Ancillary Relief) as set out in the Schedule to these Rules; and

    (b)     after Form H insert Form H1 (Statement of Costs (Ancillary Relief)) as set out in the Schedule to these Rules.

**10 Transitional provision**

The 1991 Rules shall apply to—

    (a)     an application for ancillary relief made in a petition or answer before these Rules come into force;

(b)     an application for ancillary relief made in Form A before these Rules come into force (no such application having been made in the petition or answer); or

(c)     an application under section 10(2) of the Matrimonial Causes Act 1973([2]) or an application under section 48(2) of the Civil Partnership Act 2004([3]) made in Form B before these Rules come into force,

as if these Rules had not been made.

---

[2]   1973 c.18.
[3]   2004 c.33.

**SCHEDULE     RULE 9**

Form H                                                    rule 2.61F(1)

# Estimate of Costs (Ancillary Relief) of

| In the | |
|---|---|
| | **\*[County Court]** <br> **\*[Principal Registry of the Family Division]** |
| **Case No.** <br> *Always quote this* | |
| Applicant's Solicitor's reference | |
| Respondent's Solicitor's reference | |

*(\*delete as appropriate)*

*(name of party)*

the   Applicant  ☐
        Resondent  ☐

**Between**

**and**

Estimate of costs relating to ancillary relief application for hearing on: [                    ]

**Please Note: it is a requirement of the rules to provide full costs information to the court**

*(Do not include here costs incurred in respect of other aspects of the case, for example, the divorce or civil partnership proceedings, children matters, injunctions, etc.)*

### SUMMARY OF COSTS ESTIMATE

| | Prescribed rates for publicly funded services £ | Indemnity Rate £ |
|---|---|---|
| **GRAND TOTAL** <br> **(Box 7 + Box 14)** | | |
| State what has been paid towards the grand total above. | | |
| Amount of any contributions paid by the funded client towards their publicly funded services. | | |

Signature of solicitor:
(or party, if not represented)  [                    ]     Dated: [                    ]

Name of firm of solicitors: [                    ]     Ref: [                    ]

The court office at

is open between 10 am and 4 pm (4.30pm at the Principal Registry of the Family Division) Monday to Friday. When corresponding with the court, please address forms or letters to the Court Manager and quote the case number. If you do not do so, your correspondence may be returned.

**Form H** Estimate of Costs (Ancillary Relief) (03.06)                                    HMCS

**SECTION A:**
Costs incurred in the Ancillary Relief proceedings **prior** to issue of Form A

**PART 1**

| | Prescribed rates for publicly funded services £ | Indemnity Rate £ |
|---|---|---|
| 1. Ancillary Relief solicitors' costs (including VAT) incurred by any previous solicitors. | | |
| 2. Ancillary Relief solicitors' costs (including VAT) incurred by the current solicitors. | | |
| 3. Disbursements (including VAT, if appropriate) incurred by any previous solicitors. | | |
| 4. Disbursements (including VAT, if appropriate) incurred by current solicitors. | | |
| 5. All counsel's fees (including VAT). | | |
| **SUB-TOTAL** | | |

**PART 2**

| | | |
|---|---|---|
| 6. Add any private client costs previously incurred (in publicly funded cases only) | | |
| 7. **TOTAL OF SECTION A** | | |

**SECTION B:**
Costs incurred in the Ancillary Relief proceedings **after** issue of Form A

**PART 3**

| | Prescribed rates for publicly funded services £ | Indemnity Rate £ |
|---|---|---|
| 8. Ancillary Relief solicitors' costs (including VAT) incurred by any previous solicitors. | | |
| 9. Ancillary Relief solicitors' costs (including VAT and costs of the current hearing) incurred by the current solicitors. | | |
| 10. Disbursements (including VAT, if appropriate) incurred by any previous solicitors. | | |
| 11. Disbursements (including VAT, if appropriate) incurred by current solicitors. | | |
| 12. All counsel's fees (including VAT). | | |
| **SUB-TOTAL** | | |

**PART 4**

| | | |
|---|---|---|
| 13. Add any private client costs previously incurred (in publicly funded cases only). | | |
| 14. **TOTAL OF SECTION B** | | |

Form H1                                                         rule 2.61F(2)

## Statement of Costs (Ancillary Relief) of

| In the |
|---|
| **\*[County Court]** |
| **\*[Principal Registry of the Family Division]** |

| Case No. *Always quote this* | |
|---|---|
| Applicant's Solicitor's reference | |
| Respondent's Solicitor's reference | |

*(\*delete as appropriate)*

*(name of party)*

the    Applicant  ☐

       Resondent  ☐

**Between**

**and**

Statement of costs relating to ancillary relief application for hearing on: [               ]

**Please Note: it is a requirement of the rules to provide full costs information to the court**

*(Do not include in this form costs incurred in respect of other aspects of the case, for example, the divorce or civil partnership proceedings, children matters, injunctions, etc.)*

Description of fee earner:

(a) Name:                         Status:             Hourly Rate Claimed: £

(b) Name:                         Status:             Hourly Rate Claimed: £

(c) Name:                         Status:             Hourly Rate Claimed: £

(d) Name:                         Status:             Hourly Rate Claimed: £

### SUMMARY OF COSTS STATEMENT

| | Prescribed rates for publicly funded services £ | Indemnity Rate £ |
|---|---|---|
| **TOTAL SECTION A (Box 7)** | | |
| **TOTAL SECTION B (Box 14)** | | |
| **TOTAL SECTION C (Box 21)** | | |
| **TOTAL SECTION D (Box 25)** | | |
| **TOTAL SECTION E (Box 26)** (if completed) | | |
| **GRAND TOTAL (A +B +C + D + E)** | | |
| State what has been paid towards the grand total above. | | |
| Amount of any contributions paid by the funded client towards their publicly funded services. | | |

Signature of solicitor:                        Dated:
(or party, if not represented)

Name of firm of solicitors:                        Ref:

The court office at

is open between 10 am and 4 pm (4.30pm at the Principal Registry of the Family Division) Monday to Friday. When corresponding with the court, please address forms or letters to the Court Manager and quote the case number. If you do not do so, your correspondence may be returned.

**SECTION A:**
Costs incurred in the Ancillary Relief proceedings **prior** to issue of Form A

**PART 1**

| | Prescribed rates for publicly funded services £ | Indemnity Rate £ |
|---|---|---|
| 1. Ancillary Relief solicitors' costs (including VAT) incurred by any previous solicitors. | | |
| 2. Ancillary Relief solicitors' costs (including VAT) incurred by the current solicitors. | | |
| 3. Disbursements (including VAT, if appropriate) incurred by any previous solicitors. | | |
| 4. Disbursements (including VAT, if appropriate) incurred by current solicitors. | | |
| 5. All counsel's fees (including VAT). | | |
| **SUB-TOTAL** | | |

**PART 2**

| | | |
|---|---|---|
| 6. Add any private client costs previously incurred (in publicly funded cases only) | | |

| | | |
|---|---|---|
| 7. **TOTAL OF SECTION A** | | |

**SECTION B:**
Costs incurred in the Ancillary Relief proceedings **after** issue of Form A up to and including FDR appointment (or, if none, the date of the last Form H)

**PART 3**

| | Prescribed rates for publicly funded services £ | Indemnity Rate £ |
|---|---|---|
| 8. Ancillary Relief solicitors' costs (including VAT) incurred by any previous solicitors. | | |
| 9. Ancillary Relief solicitors' costs (including VAT) incurred by the current solicitors. | | |
| 10. Disbursements (including VAT, if appropriate) incurred by any previous solicitors. | | |
| 11. Disbursements (including VAT, if appropriate) incurred by current solicitors. | | |
| 12. All counsel's fees (including VAT). | | |
| **SUB-TOTAL** | | |

**PART 4**

| | | |
|---|---|---|
| 13. Add any private client costs previously incurred (in publicly funded cases only). | | |

| | | |
|---|---|---|
| 14. **TOTAL OF SECTION B** | | |

2

**SECTION C:**

Costs incurred in the Ancillary Relief proceedings **after** FDR appointment (or, if none, the date of the last Form H) up to the date of this form.

**PART 5**

| | Prescribed rates for publicly funded services £ | Indemnity Rate £ |
|---|---|---|
| 15. Ancillary Relief solicitors' costs (including VAT) incurred by any previous solicitors. | | |
| 16. Ancillary Relief solicitors' costs (including VAT) incurred by the current solicitors. | | |
| 17. Disbursements (including VAT, if appropriate) incurred by any previous solicitors. | | |
| 18. Disbursements (including VAT, if appropriate) incurred by current solicitors. | | |
| 19. All counsel's fees (including VAT). (Counsel's fees for final hearing should not be included here, but given in Section D.) | | |
| **SUB-TOTAL** | | |

**PART 6**

| | | |
|---|---|---|
| 20. Add any private client costs previously incurred (in publicly funded cases only). | | |
| 21. **TOTAL OF SECTION C** | | |

**SECTION D:**

Estimate of costs expected and incurred in the Ancillary Relief proceedings **after** the date of this form up to the end of the final hearing.

**PART 7**

| | Prescribed rates for publicly funded services £ | Indemnity Rate £ |
|---|---|---|
| 22. Ancillary Relief solicitors' costs (including VAT) | | |
| 23. Disbursements (including VAT, if appropriate) | | |
| 24. Counsel's fees (including VAT). (All counsel's fees expected to be incurred for final hearing should be included here.) | | |
| 25. **TOTAL OF SECTION D** | | |

**SECTION E:**

Estimate of costs to be incurred in implementing proposed order for ancillary relief.

*(Note: Include only those costs which it is known or anticipated will be incurred in giving effect to the order.*
*If the work to be carried out is only conveyancing, the prescribed rates for public funding services do not apply.)*

**PART 8**

| | Prescribed rates for publicly funded services £ | Indemnity Rate £ |
|---|---|---|
| 26. **TOTAL OF SECTION E** (Total estimate costs of implementing prosed order) | | |

# PRACTICE DIRECTION ABOUT COSTS

## Supplementing CPR Parts 43–48 (PD Costs)

\*\*\*\*

### SECTION 8 – COURT'S DISCRETION AND CIRCUMSTANCES TO BE TAKEN INTO ACCOUNT WHEN EXERCISING ITS DISCRETION AS TO COSTS: RULE 44.3

8.1 Attention is drawn to the factors set out in this rule which may lead the court to depart from the general rule stated in rule 44.3(2) and to make a different order about costs.

8.2 In a probate claim where a defendant has in his defence given notice that he requires the will to be proved in solemn form (see paragraph 8.3 of the Contentious Probate practice direction supplementing Part 49), the court will not make an order for costs against the defendant unless it appears that there was no reasonable ground for opposing the will. The term 'probate claim' is defined in paragraph 1.2 of the Contentious Probate practice direction.

8.3

(1) The court may make an order about costs at any stage in a case.

(2) In particular the court may make an order about costs when it deals with any application, makes any order or holds any hearing and that order about costs may relate to the costs of that application, order or hearing.

(3) Rule 44.3A(1) provides that the court will not assess any additional liability until the conclusion of the proceedings or the part of the proceedings to which the funding arrangement relates. (Paras 2.4 and 2.5 above explain when proceedings are concluded. As to the time when detailed assessment may be carried out see para 28.1, below.)

8.4 In deciding what order to make about costs the court is required to have regard to all the circumstances including any payment into court or admissible offer to settle made by a party which is drawn to the court's attention (whether or not it is made in accordance with Part 36). Where a claimant has made a Part 36 offer and fails to obtain a judgment which is more advantageous than that offer, that circumstance alone will not lead to a reduction in the costs awarded to the claimant under this rule.

8.5 There are certain costs orders which the court will commonly make in proceedings before trial. The following table sets out the general effect of these orders. The table is not an exhaustive list of the orders which the court may make.

| Term | Effect |
| --- | --- |
| Costs<br><br>Costs in any event | The party in whose favour the order is made is entitled to the costs in respect of the part of the proceedings to which the order relates, whatever other costs orders are made in the proceedings. |
| Costs in the case<br><br>Costs in the application | The party in whose favour the court makes an order for costs at the end of the proceedings is entitled to his costs of the part of the proceedings to which the order relates. |

| Term | Effect |
|------|--------|
| Costs reserved | The decision about costs is deferred to a later occasion, but if no later order is made the costs will be costs in the case. |
| Claimant's/ defendant's costs in the case/ application | If the party in whose favour the costs order is made is awarded costs at the end of the proceedings, that party is entitled to his costs of the part of the proceedings to which the order relates. If any other party is awarded costs at the end of the proceedings, the party in whose favour the final costs order is made is not liable to pay the costs of any other party in respect of the part of the proceedings to which the order relates. |
| Costs thrown away | Where, for example, a judgment or order is set aside, the party in whose favour the costs order is made is entitled to the costs which have been incurred as a consequence. This includes the costs of –<br><br>(a) preparing for and attending any hearing at which the judgment or order which has been set aside was made;<br><br>(b) preparing for and attending any hearing to set aside the judgment or order in question;<br><br>(c) preparing for and attending any hearing at which the court orders the proceedings or the part in question to be adjourned;<br><br>(d) any steps taken to enforce a judgment or order which has subsequently been set aside. |
| Costs of and caused by | Where, for example, the court makes this order on an application to amend a statement of case, the party in whose favour the costs order is made is entitled to the costs of preparing for and attending the application and the costs of any consequential amendment to his own statement of case. |
| Costs here and below | The party in whose favour the costs order is made is entitled not only to his costs in respect of the proceedings in which the court makes the order but also to his costs of the proceedings in any lower court. In the case of an appeal from a Divisional Court the party is not entitled to any costs incurred in any court below the Divisional Court. |
| No order as to costs<br><br>Each party to pay his own costs | Each party is to bear his own costs of the part of the proceedings to which the order relates whatever costs order the court makes at the end of the proceedings. |

8.6 Where, under rule 44.3(8), the court orders an amount to be paid before costs are assessed –

    (1)    the order will state that amount, and

    (2)    if no other date for payment is specified in the order rule 44.8 (Time for complying with an order for costs) will apply.

**Fees of counsel**

8.7

(1) This paragraph applies where the court orders the detailed assessment of the costs of a hearing at which one or more counsel appeared for a party.

(2) Where an order for costs states the opinion of the court as to whether or not the hearing was fit for the attendance of one or more counsel, a costs officer conducting a detailed assessment of costs to which that order relates will have regard to the opinion stated.

(3) The court will generally express an opinion only where –

    (a)    the paying party asks it to do so;

    (b)    more than one counsel appeared for the party or,

    (c)    the court wishes to record its opinion that the case was not fit for the attendance of counsel.

**Fees payable to conveyancing counsel appointed by the court to assist it**

8.8

(1) Where the court refers any matter to the conveyancing counsel of the court the fees payable to counsel in respect of the work done or to be done will be assessed by the court in accordance with rule 44.3.

(2) An appeal from a decision of the court in respect of the fees of such counsel will be dealt with under the general rules as to appeals set out in Part 52. If the appeal is against the decision of an authorised court officer, it will be dealt with in accordance with rules 47.20 to 47.23.

****

## SECTION 11 – FACTORS TO BE TAKEN INTO ACCOUNT IN DECIDING THE AMOUNT OF COSTS: RULE 44.5

11.1 In applying the test of proportionality the court will have regard to rule 1.1(2)(c). The relationship between the total of the costs incurred and the financial value of the claim may not be a reliable guide. A fixed percentage cannot be applied in all cases to the value of the claim in order to ascertain whether or not the costs are proportionate.

11.2 In any proceedings there will be costs which will inevitably be incurred and which are necessary for the successful conduct of the case. Solicitors are not required to conduct litigation at rates which are uneconomic. Thus in a modest claim the proportion of costs is likely to be higher than in a large claim, and may even equal or possibly exceed the amount in dispute.

11.3 Where a trial takes place, the time taken by the court in dealing with a particular issue may not be an accurate guide to the amount of time properly spent by the legal or other representatives in preparation for the trial of that issue.

11.4 Where a party has entered into a funding arrangement the costs claimed may, subject to rule 44.3B include an additional liability.

11.5 In deciding whether the costs claimed are reasonable and (on a standard basis assessment) proportionate, the court will consider the amount of any additional liability separately from the base costs.

11.6 In deciding whether the base costs are reasonable and (if relevant) proportionate the court will consider the factors set out in rule 44.5.

11.7 Subject to paragraph 17.8(2), when the court is considering the factors to be taken into account in assessing an additional liability, it will have regard to the facts and circumstances as they reasonably appeared to the solicitor or counsel when the funding arrangement was entered into and at the time of any variation of the arrangement.

11.8

(1) In deciding whether a percentage increase is reasonable relevant factors to be taken into account may include –

    (a)    the risk that the circumstances in which the costs, fees or expenses would be payable might or might not occur;

    (b)    the legal representative's liability for any disbursements;

    (c)    what other methods of financing the costs were available to the receiving party.

11.9 A percentage increase will not be reduced simply on the ground that, when added to base costs which are reasonable and (where relevant) proportionate, the total appears disproportionate.

11.10 In deciding whether the cost of insurance cover is reasonable, relevant factors to be taken into account include:

    (1)    where the insurance cover is not purchased in support of a conditional fee agreement with a success fee, how its cost compares with the likely cost of funding the case with a conditional fee agreement with a success fee and supporting insurance cover;

    (2)    the level and extent of the cover provided;

    (3)    the availability of any pre-existing insurance cover;

    (4)    whether any part of the premium would be rebated in the event of early settlement;

    (5)    the amount of commission payable to the receiving party or his legal representatives or other agents.

11.11 Where the court is considering a provision made by a membership organisation, rule 44.3B(1)(b) provides that any such provision which exceeds the likely cost to the receiving party of the premium of an insurance policy against the risk of incurring a liability to pay the costs of other parties to the proceedings is not recoverable. In such circumstances the court will, when assessing the additional liability, have regard to the factors set out in paragraph 11.10 above, in addition to the factors set out in rule 44.5.

****

## SECTION 18 – COURT'S POWERS IN RELATION TO MISCONDUCT: RULE 44.14

18.1 Before making an order under rule 44.14 the court must give the party or legal representative in question a reasonable opportunity to attend a hearing to give reasons why it should not make such an order.

18.2 Conduct before or during the proceedings which gave rise to the assessment which is unreasonable or improper includes steps which are calculated to prevent or inhibit the court from furthering the overriding objective.

18.3 Although rule 44.14(3) does not specify any sanction for breach of the obligation imposed by the rule the court may, either in the order under paragraph (2) or in a subsequent order, require the solicitor to produce to the court evidence that he took reasonable steps to comply with the obligation.

****

## SECTION 53 – PERSONAL LIABILITY OF LEGAL REPRESENTATIVE FOR COSTS – WASTED COSTS ORDERS: RULE 48.7

53.1 Rule 48.7 deals with wasted costs orders against legal representatives. Such orders can be made at any stage in the proceedings up to and including the proceedings relating to the detailed assessment of costs. In general, applications for wasted costs are best left until after the end of the trial.

53.2 The court may make a wasted costs order against a legal representative on its own initiative.

53.3 A party may apply for a wasted costs order –

    (1)    by filing an application notice in accordance with Part 23; or

    (2)    by making an application orally in the course of any hearing.

53.4 It is appropriate for the court to make a wasted costs order against a legal representative, only if –

    (1)    the legal representative has acted improperly, unreasonably or negligently;

    (2)    his conduct has caused a party to incur unnecessary costs; and

    (3)    it is just in all the circumstances to order him to compensate that party for the whole or part of those costs.

53.5 The court will give directions about the procedure that will be followed in each case in order to ensure that the issues are dealt with in a way which is fair and as simple and summary as the circumstances permit.

53.6 As a general rule the court will consider whether to make a wasted costs order in two stages –

    (1)    in the first stage, the court must be satisfied –

        (a)    that it has before it evidence or other material which, if unanswered, would be likely to lead to a wasted costs order being made; and

        (b)    the wasted costs proceedings are justified notwithstanding the likely costs involved.

    (2)    at the second stage (even if the court is satisfied under paragraph (1)) the court will consider, after giving the legal representative an opportunity to give reasons why the court should not make a wasted costs order, whether it is appropriate to make a wasted costs order in accordance with paragraph 53.4 above.

53.7 On an application for a wasted costs order under Part 23 the court may proceed to the second stage described in paragraph 53.6 without first adjourning the hearing if it is satisfied that the legal representative has already had a reasonable opportunity to give reasons why the court should not make a wasted costs order. In other cases the court will adjourn the hearing before proceeding to the second stage.

53.8 On an application for a wasted costs order under Part 23 the application notice and any evidence in support must identify –

    (1)    what the legal representative is alleged to have done or failed to do; and

  (2)  the costs that he may be ordered to pay or which are sought against him.

53.9  A wasted costs order is an order –

  (1)  that the legal representative pay a specified sum in respect of costs to a party; or

  (2)  for costs relating to a specified sum or items of work to be disallowed.

53.10 Attention is drawn to rule 44.3A(1) and (2) which respectively prevent the court from assessing any additional liability until the conclusion of the proceedings (or the part of the proceedings) to which the funding arrangement relates, and set out the orders the court may make at the conclusion of the proceedings.

****

# PRESIDENT'S DIRECTION

# 25 MAY 2000

**Citation:** [2000] 1 FLR 997

# ANCILLARY RELIEF PROCEDURE

1 Introduction

1.1 The Family Proceedings (Amendment No 2) Rules 1999 make important amendments to the Family Proceedings Rules 1991 as from 5 June 2000. The existing 'pilot scheme' rules in relation to ancillary relief which have applied since 1996 but only in specified courts will become, with significant revisions, of general application. In the same way as the pilot scheme, the new procedure is intended to reduce delay, facilitate settlements, limit costs incurred by parties and provide the court with greater and more effective control over the conduct of the proceedings.

2 Pre-application Protocol

2.1 The 'Pre-application protocol' annexed to this Direction outlines the steps parties should take to seek and provide information from and to each other prior to the commencement of any ancillary relief application. The court will expect the parties to comply with the terms of the protocol.

3 Financial Dispute Resolution (FDR) Appointment

3.1 A key element in the new procedure is the Financial Dispute Resolution (FDR) appointment. Rule 2.61E provides that the FDR appointment is to be treated as a meeting held for the purposes of discussion and negotiation. Such meetings which were previously described as meetings held for the purposes of conciliation have been developed as a means of reducing the tension which inevitably arises in matrimonial and family disputes and facilitating settlement of those disputes.

3.2 In order for the FDR appointment to be effective, parties must approach the occasion openly and without reserve. Non-disclosure of the content of such meetings is accordingly vital and is an essential prerequisite for fruitful discussion directed to the settlement of the dispute between the parties. The FDR appointment is an important part of the settlement process. As a consequence of *Re D (Minors) (Conciliation: Disclosure of Information)* [1993] Fam 231, sub nom *Re D (Minors) (Conciliation: Privilege)* [1993] 1 FLR 932, evidence of anything said or of any admission made in the course of an FDR appointment will not be admissible in evidence, except at the trial of a person for an offence committed at the appointment or in the very exceptional circumstances indicated in *Re D*.

3.3 Courts will therefore expect:

> parties to make offers and proposals;
>
> recipients of offers and proposals to give them proper consideration;

that parties, whether separately or together, will not seek to exclude from consideration at the appointment any such offer or proposal.

3.4 In order to make the most effective use of the first appointment and the FDR appointment, the legal representatives attending those appointments will be expected to have full knowledge of the case.

4 Single joint expert

4.1 The introduction of expert evidence in proceedings is likely to increase costs substantially and consequently the court will use its powers to restrict the unnecessary use of experts. Accordingly, where expert evidence is sought to be relied upon, parties should if possible agree upon a single expert whom they can jointly instruct. Where parties are unable to agree upon the expert to be instructed, the court will consider using its powers under Part 35 of the Civil Procedure Rules 1998 to direct that evidence be given by one expert only. In such cases parties must be in a position at the first appointment or when the matter comes to be considered by the court to provide the court with a list of suitable experts or to make submissions as to the method by which the expert is to be selected.

5 This Direction shall have effect as from 5 June 2000 and replaces *Practice Direction: Ancillary Relief Procedure: Pilot Scheme* [1997] 2 FLR 304 dated 16 June 1997.

6 Issued with the approval and concurrence of the Lord Chancellor.

Dame Elizabeth Butler-Sloss
*President*

## PRE-APPLICATION PROTOCOL

1 *Introduction*

1.1

    1.1.1    Lord Woolf in his final *Access to Justice* Report of July 1996 recommended the development of pre-application protocols:

        'to build on and increase the benefits of early but well informed settlement which genuinely satisfy both parties to dispute'

    1.1.2    Subsequently, in April 2000 the Lord Chancellor's Ancillary Relief Advisory Committee agreed this Pre-application Protocol.

1.2 The aim of the pre-application protocol is to ensure that:

    (*a*)    pre-application disclosure and negotiation takes place in appropriate cases;

    (*b*)    where there is pre-application disclosure and negotiation, it is dealt with:

        (i)    cost-effectively;

        (ii)    in line with the overriding objectives of the Family Proceedings (Amendments) Rules 1999;

    (*c*)    the parties are in a position to settle the case fairly and early without litigation.

1.3 The court will be able to treat the standard set in the pre-application protocol as the normal reasonable approach to pre-application conduct. If proceedings are subsequently issued, the court will be entitled to decide whether there has been non-compliance with the protocol and, if so, whether non-compliance merits consequences.

2 *Notes of guidance*

## Scope of the Protocol

2.1 This protocol is intended to apply to all claims for ancillary relief as defined by FPR 1991, r 1(2). It is designed to cover all classes of case, ranging from a simple application for periodical payments to an application for a substantial lump sum and property adjustment order. The protocol is designed to facilitate the operation of what was called the pilot scheme and is from 5 June 2000 the standard procedure for ancillary relief applications.

2.2 In considering the option of pre-application disclosure and negotiation, solicitors should bear in mind the advantage of having a court timetable and court-managed process. There is sometimes an advantage in preparing disclosure before proceedings are commenced. However, solicitors should bear in mind the objective of controlling costs and in particular the costs of discovery and that the option of pre-application disclosure and negotiation has risks of excessive and uncontrolled expenditure and delay. This option should only be encouraged where both parties agree to follow this route and disclosure is not likely to be an issue or has been adequately dealt with in mediation or otherwise.

2.3 Solicitors should consider at an early stage and keep under review whether it would be appropriate to suggest mediation to the clients as an alternative to solicitor negotiation or court-based litigation.

2.4 Making an application to the court should not be regarded as a hostile step or a last resort, rather as a way of starting the court timetable, controlling disclosure and endeavouring to avoid the costly final hearing and the preparation for it.

## First letter

2.5 The circumstances of parties to an application for ancillary relief are so various that it would be difficult to prepare a specimen first letter. The request for information will be different in every case. However, the tone of the initial letter is important and the guidelines in para 3.7 should be followed. It should be approved in advance by the client. Solicitors writing to an unrepresented party should always recommend that he seeks independent legal advice and enclose a second copy of the letter to be passed to any solicitor instructed. A reasonable time-limit for a response may be 14 days.

## Negotiation and settlement

2.6 In the event of pre-application disclosure and negotiation, as envisaged in para 2.2 an application should not be issued when a settlement is a reasonable prospect.

## Disclosure

2.7 The protocol underlines the obligation of parties to make full and frank disclosure of all material facts, documents and other information relevant to the issues. Solicitors owe their clients a duty to tell them in clear terms of this duty and of the possible consequences of breach of the duty. This duty of disclosure is an ongoing obligation and includes the duty to disclose any material changes after initial disclosure has been given. Solicitors are referred to the *Good Practice Guide for Disclosure* produced by the Solicitors Family Law Association (obtainable from the Administrative Director, 366A Crofton Road, Orpington, Kent BR2 8NN).

3 *The Protocol*

## General principles

3.1 All parties must always bear in mind the overriding objective set out at FPR 1991, r 2.51B and try to ensure that all claims should be resolved and a just outcome achieved as speedily as possible without costs being unreasonably incurred. The needs of any children should be addressed and safeguarded. The procedures which it is appropriate to follow should be conducted with minimum distress to the parties and in a manner designed to promote as good a continuing relationship between the parties and any children affected as is possible in the circumstances.

3.2 The principle of proportionality must be borne in mind at all times. It is unacceptable for the costs of any case to be disproportionate to the financial value of the subject matter of the dispute.

3.3 Parties should be informed that where a court exercises a discretion as to whether costs are payable by one party to another, this discretion extends to pre-application offers to settle and conduct of disclosure (r 44.3, para 1 of the Civil Procedure Rules 1998).

### Identifying the issues

3.4 Parties must seek to clarify their claims and identify the issues between them as soon as possible. So that this can be achieved they must provide full, frank and clear disclosure of facts, information and documents which are material and sufficiently accurate to enable proper negotiations to take place to settle their differences. Openness in all dealings is essential.

### Disclosure

3.5 If parties carry out voluntary disclosure before the issue of proceedings the parties should exchange schedules of assets, income, liabilities and other material facts, using Form E as a guide to the format of the disclosure. Documents should only be disclosed to the extent that they are required by Form E. Excessive or disproportionate costs should not be incurred.

### Correspondence

3.6 Any first letter and subsequent correspondence must focus on the clarification of claims and identification of issues and their resolution. Protracted and unnecessary correspondence and 'trial by correspondence' must be avoided.

3.7 The impact of any correspondence upon the reader and in particular the parties must always be considered. Any correspondence which raises irrelevant issues or which might cause the other party to adopt an entrenched, polarised or hostile position is to be discouraged.

### Experts

3.8 Expert valuation evidence is only necessary where the parties cannot agree or do not know the value of some significant asset. The cost of a valuation should be proportionate to the sums in dispute. Wherever possible, valuations of properties, shares, etc should be obtained from a single valuer instructed by both parties. To that end, a party wishing to instruct an expert (the first party) should first give the other party a list of the names of one or more experts in the relevant speciality whom he considers are suitable to instruct. Within 14 days the other party may indicate an objection to one or more of the named experts and, if so, should supply the names of one or more experts whom he considers suitable.

3.9 Where the identity of the expert is agreed, the parties should agree the terms of a joint letter of instructions.

3.10 Where no agreement is reached as to the identity of the expert, each party should think carefully before instructing his own expert because of the costs implications. Disagreements about disclosure such as the use and identity of an expert may be better managed by the court within the context of an application for ancillary relief.

3.11 Whether a joint report is commissioned or the parties have chosen to instruct separate experts, it is important that the expert is prepared to answer reasonable questions raised by either party.

3.12 When experts' reports are commissioned pre-application, it should be made clear to the expert that they may in due course be reporting to the court and that they should therefore consider themselves bound by the guidance as to expert witnesses in Part 35 of the Civil Procedure Rules 1998.

3.13 Where the parties propose to instruct a joint expert, there is a duty on both parties to disclose whether they have already consulted that expert about the assets in issue.

3.14 If the parties agree to instruct separate experts the parties should be encouraged to agree in advance that the reports will be disclosed.

**Summary**

3.15 The aim of all pre-application proceedings steps must be to assist the parties to resolve their differences speedily and fairly or at least narrow the issues and, should that not be possible, to assist the court to do so.

# PRESIDENT'S DIRECTION

## 24 JULY 2000

**Citation:** [2000] 2 FLR 428

# COSTS: CIVIL PROCEDURE RULES 1998

The President's Direction: Civil Procedure Rules 1998: Allocation of Cases: Costs [1999] 1 FLR 1295 dated 22 April 1999 applied the (Civil Procedure) Practice Direction about costs Supplementing Parts 43 to 48 of the Civil Procedure Rules ('the costs direction') to family proceedings (within the Family Proceedings Rules 1991) and to proceedings in the Family Division. A further edition of the costs direction (effective from 3 July 2000) has been published and it is hereby directed that the further edition (and all subsequent editions as and when they are published and come into effect) shall extend to family proceedings and to proceedings in the Family Division in the same way as did the costs direction and to the extent applicable to such proceedings.

The further edition of the costs direction includes provisions applicable to proceedings following changes in the manner in which legal services are funded pursuant to the Access to Justice Act 1999. It should be noted that although the cost of the premium in respect of legal costs insurance (s 29) or the cost of funding by a prescribed membership organisation (s 30) may be recoverable, family proceedings (within s 58A(2) of the Courts and Legal Services Act 1990) cannot be the subject of an enforceable conditional fee agreement.

Issued with the approval of the Lord Chancellor.

Dame Elizabeth Butler-Sloss
*President*

# THE PRINCIPAL REGISTRY OF THE FAMILY DIVISION

# ANCILLARY RELIEF: COSTS

# PRESIDENT'S DIRECTION

# 20 FEBRUARY 2006

**Citation:** [2006] 1 FLR 864

1. The Family Proceedings (Amendment) Rules 2006 make significant changes to the court's power to make costs orders in ancillary relief proceedings. The new rules will come into force on 3rd April 2006. They will apply to an application for ancillary relief contained in a petition or answer filed on or after 3rd April 2006, or to such an application which has not been made in a petition or answer but is made in Form A on or after that date. The rules will also apply to an application under section 10(2) of the Matrimonial Causes Act 1973 or under section 48(2) of the Civil Partnership Act 2004 made in Form B on or after that date. They do not however apply to such applications if they are to be heard by the court with an application which was made before that date.

2. Under the new rules the court will only have power to make a costs order in ancillary relief proceedings when this is justified by the litigation conduct of one of the parties (see new rule 2.71 of the Family Proceedings Rules 1991). When determining whether and how to exercise this power the court will be required to take into account the list of factors set out in the rules. The court will no longer be able to take into account any offers to settle expressed to be 'without prejudice' or 'without prejudice save as to costs' in deciding what, if any, costs order to make.

3. The new rules require the completion of Forms H and H1 (see rule 2.61F of the Family Proceedings Rules 1991, as amended). Form H is to be used at interim hearings so that the court has available to it a realistic estimate of the costs incurred to date. Form H1 is for use at a final hearing to provide the court with accurate details of the costs which each party has incurred, or expects to incur, in relation to the ancillary relief proceedings. The purpose of this form is to enable the court to take account of the impact of each party's costs liability on their financial situations. Parties should ensure that the information contained in these forms is as full and accurate as possible and that any sums already paid in respect of a party's ancillary relief costs are clearly set out. Where relevant, any liability arising from the costs of other proceedings between the parties should continue to be referred to in the appropriate section of a party's Form E; any such costs should not be included in Forms H or H1.

4. Parties who intend to seek a costs order against another party in proceedings to which rule 2.71 of the Family Proceedings Rules 1991 applies should ordinarily make this plain in open correspondence or in skeleton arguments before the date of the hearing. In any case where summary assessment of costs awarded under rule 2.71 of the Family Proceedings Rules 1991 would be appropriate parties are under an obligation to file a statement of costs in CPR Form N260 (see CPR Practice Direction supplementing Parts 43 to 48 (Costs), Section 13 and paragraph 6 below).

5. An order for maintenance pending suit which includes an element to allow a party to deal with legal fees (see *A v A (maintenance pending suit: provision for legal fees)* [2001] 1 WLR 605; *G v G (maintenance pending suit: costs)* [2002] EWHC 306 (Fam); *McFarlane v McFarlane, Parlour v Parlour* [2004] EWCA Civ 872; *Moses-Taiga v Taiga* [2005] EWCA Civ 1013) is an order made pursuant to section 22 of the Matrimonial Causes Act 1973, and is not a 'costs order' within the meaning of rule 2.71 of the Family Proceedings Rules 1991.

6. The President's Direction: Civil Procedure Rules 1998: Allocation of Cases: Costs dated 22nd April 1999 (as supplemented by the President's Direction: Costs: Civil Procedure Rules 1998 dated 24th July 2000) makes provision in relation to the application of the (Civil Procedure) Practice Direction about costs (Supplementing Parts 43 to 48 of the Civil Procedure Rules) to family proceedings to which the Family Proceedings Rules 1991 apply. Those President's Directions will apply to a costs order made under new rule 2.71 of the Family Proceedings Rules 1991 as though the reference to the (Civil Procedure) Practice Direction was a reference to that direction excluding Section 6, Paragraphs 8.1 to 8.4 and Sections 15 and 16.

7. Issued with the concurrence of the Lord Chancellor.


Sir Mark Potter, P